SKINNY
SALADS

To my Mum Elsie,
my daughter Elsie
and the one and only Rich

80 flavour-packed recipes of less than 300 calories

Kathryn Bruton

Photography by Laura Edwards

Kyle Books

Nutritional information key:
DF – dairy-free
GF – gluten-free
V – vegetarian
VE – vegan

First published in Great Britain in 2017 by
Kyle Books, an imprint of Kyle Cathie Ltd
192–198 Vauxhall Bridge Road
London SW1V 1DX
general.enquiries@kylebooks.com
www.kylebooks.co.uk

10 9 8 7 6 5 4 3 2 1

ISBN 978 0 85783 368 6

Project Editor: Claire Rogers
Copy Editor: Anne McDowall
Designer: Louise Leffler
Photographer: Laura Edwards
Food Stylist: Kathryn Bruton
Prop Stylist: Tab Hawkins
Production: Nic Jones, Gemma John and Lisa Pinnell

A Cataloguing in Publication record for this title
is available from the British Library.

Colour reproduction by f1 colour
Printed and bound in China by 1010 Printing
International Ltd

contents

introduction

Salads suffer from stereotypes, but this couldn't be further from the truth. When I began writing this book, my goal was to create salad recipes good enough to eat at any time of year, on any occasion, for any meal of the day, all containing less than 300 calories per serving and all packed with flavour, goodness and nutrition. Most importantly, I wanted these salads to be substantial enough to satisfy, whether eaten for breakfast, lunch, dinner or dessert.

I always endeavour to find ways of eating what I love in a healthier way and I am a firm believer that low-calorie meal options should be as flavoursome, satisfying and indulgent as any other. I met with a dubious audience when I set out to create a blue cheese dressing to feature in this book ('that salad will never be less than 300 calories!'). Could a Panzanella, bursting with tomato, basil and chunky bread, or a salad adorned with silky, succulent salami fit into this book? Would a crispy duck salad with a luscious plum dressing belong? Creating low-calorie, healthy recipes is about using the ingredients you love, even the most indulgent ones, playing around with quantities and balance, all while striving to create a dish that will not make you feel like you are missing out on something better.

I love food — all food, from creamy cheeses to indulgent charcuterie, crusty bread and carby pasta. I also love fresh vibrant fruit and vegetables, and the array of grains and pulses available makes me joyful. I couldn't pick a favourite between meat, poultry, fish and game. It is my love of all things naughty and nice coupled with my desire to be healthy

that drives me to create recipes that allow me, and you, to have it all. And so I tested and retested until I found a way to create a beautifully tasty blue cheese dressing, to include salami in a salad that contains a mere 130 calories per portion, to have a decadent panzanella and a crispy duck salad both coming in under 200 calories per portion, and to come up with recipes that satisfy carb cravings and allow for a little indulgence.

Salads are often viewed as spring and summer dishes, offering lighter, refreshing options in warmer weather; while this is true, throughout the year their versatility knows no bounds. Comfort Salads challenges this stereotype – a collection of recipes designed for colder days when your soul needs a little tender loving care. The Classics are some of my all-time favourites, and I have given some of the more high-calorie offenders a healthy makeover. Salads are perfect to create spectacular displays of fantastically fresh and vibrant ingredients, and the Show-off chapter is full of low-calorie showstoppers. Salads are among the most effortless dishes to create, but the simplest ones get their very own chapter, as do salads in which fruit plays a starring role.

Salads, so full of possibility and potential, created with almost any ingredient you can think of, can be the healthiest of options, while being satisfying, energising and even comforting. A salad can, quite literally, be anything you want it to be. It is endlessly versatile, and I have so loved exploring how it can be so much more than I ever dreamed it could be.

the rules

There are a few essential tools and tips you need to be armed with when making salads, and these golden nuggets of knowledge will make creating salads successful and seamless.

Your ingredients must be as fresh as possible: they are the star of the show, and tired, lifeless ingredients will create the kind of salads you simply will not enjoy eating.

Your ingredients may look clean, but the fact is, you don't know what their path to your kitchen has been. Fill your sink with ice-cold water and give your leaves, herbs, fruit and vegetables a good wash.

Invest in a salad spinner: it's hard to get leaves dry once they have been soaked in water, and this genius piece of equipment makes it effortless.

Never be tempted to dress lettuce leaves that are wet or your salad will be sad and sloppy, and you will be sorry you tried to take a shortcut!

Although there are salads in this book (e.g. Roasted Vegetable and Giant Couscous, see page 66) that won't be ruined by the dressing if not eaten immediately, it is generally best to dress your salad just before serving.

If you want to save any undressed salad or leftover leaves, place them in a bowl or Tupperware box, cover with a few sheets of kitchen paper and dampen with cold water. This will help keep your salad fresh and crisp for a couple of days. Likewise, you can wrap herbs in damp kitchen paper to extend their shelf life.

To help revive leaves that are beginning to look a little sad, fill a big bowl with ice-cold water and soak your leaves for a few minutes.

know your leaves

It always amazes me the range of complex and unique flavours there is to be found in lettuce leaves: each type has its own personality, with characteristics that are individual and distinctive. Getting to know your leaves will help you to choose the most suitable ones for a particular salad. This is not an extensive list, but it does cover the leaves used in the recipes in this book and those you are most likely to come across in your local supermarkets and shops. Bags of salad leaves are a great option; just ensure they are as fresh and crisp as possible.

baby gem and romaine or cos

These leaves have a wonderful texture and a distinct but subtle flavour. They are a great all-rounder for salads and can stand up to delicate and robust dressings alike.

radicchio, chicory

Something of an acquired taste, these leaves have a fabulously bitter flavour. Dressings sweetened with honey or maple syrup bring out the best in them, as do creamy, cheesy dressings.

rocket and watercress

A bite of one of these little leaves will make your tongue tingle: their punchy, peppery hit dispels any myth that salad leaves are bland or tasteless.

land cress

This leaf has the same peppery notes as rocket and watercress, but is far more intense. If you can't find it, a mixture of watercress and rocket is a good substitute.

spinach

A handful of spinach will enhance any salad. The beautifully tender leaves are sweet but earthy, boasting an unexpected depth of flavour.

red and green oak leaf lettuce

These leaves are silky soft and delicately sweet and nutty in flavour: one of my favourites.

pak choi

You don't often see pak choi used as a salad leaf, which is a shame because it couldn't be more fit for purpose. I like to slice it lengthways or shred it. It adds the most wonderful crunch to salads. If you can find baby pak choi, give this a try, too.

butterhead lettuce

This can be green or a beautiful deep purple. It is soft, sweet, tender and a great all-rounder.

iceberg

This leaf is simply awesome. It is crunchy, satisfyingly juicy and does not deserve its reputation for being insipid. Where many leaves are earthy and pungent, iceberg is vibrantly sweet and succulent. My favourite way to serve it is in wedges.

lollo rosso

The crisp and crinkled leaves of this lettuce hold onto dressing beautifully. It is a great leafy salad option and wonderful for creating texture, too.

baby leaves

Often sold in bags in supermarkets, baby leaves are wonderfully sweet and tender and make for a great green salad (see page 21).

pea shoots

Although you are more likely to find these when they are in season, bigger supermarkets tend to stock them all year round now. Just as you would imagine, they are sweet with the essence of peas.

frisée

A member of the chicory family and similarly bitter in taste, frisée has wonderful texture. It makes a great addition to mixed salads and is delicious served with crispy pancetta and poached eggs (see page 40).

lamb's lettuce

Also knows as mache or corn salad, these leaves are very delicate, slightly tangy and nutty. Wash them very gently so as not to bruise or damage them.

grow your own sprouts

Sprouts can be an integral part of a salad or form a garnish for almost any salad you can think of. They are also an amazing little tool to add a hit of nutrition. Lots of health food shops now sell them, and you can sometimes find them in supermarkets too, but growing them at home couldn't be easier and I find it a really satisfying and rewarding thing to do. It takes only a couple of days for the seeds to sprout, so you get almost instant gratification as well as a fantastic, wholesome feeling from growing something yourself!

 Some of my recipes are delicious with a sprinkling of sprouts — look for the sprout symbol.

the equipment

You can buy sprouting jars online, but it's easy to make your own. All you need is an old jar, a bit of muslin and some string or elastic bands.

the seeds

Ensure you buy seeds that are specifically for sprouting: ask in your local health food shop. Mung beans are good ones to start with as they sprout quite quickly, which is encouraging if you are a first timer. There are loads of other types you can try though: I love mustard, radish and alfalfa. I always buy my seeds online for ease and variety.

the method

First you need to soak your seeds. Measure out no more than 2 tablespoons of seeds into your jar, cover with water and leave to soak overnight. The following morning, drain and rinse the seeds, tie the muslin cloth over the mouth of the jar and set it upside down at an angle. It needs to be in a warm place, but out of direct sunlight. Rinse the seeds at least twice a day: remove the muslin, fill the jar with water, swirl around, replace the muslin, turn the jar upside down to drain, then return it to its position. The type of seed will determine the time it takes to sprout but most will take between 2 and 5 days. When the seeds have sprouted, refrigerate and eat within 2 days.

gloriously green salads

I have kept green salads separate from the other recipes in this book because they are an accompaniment rather than a main. However, they should still be good enough to eat all on their own. The requirements are simple: fresh, crisp, seasonal leaves – and a great dressing.

Use the Know Your Leaves section (see pages 10–11) to help you choose ones that complement each other in texture and flavour and, importantly, the ones that taste great with the meal you are serving.

Meat loves the more punchy flavours of watercress and rocket, and these two leaves teamed with more subtly flavoured spinach can be the basis of a great side salad. Anything spicy will welcome juicy mellow romaine mixed with crunchy pak choi. And as a general all-rounder, baby gem and soft butterhead make a sweet, delicate salad that sits happily alongside any meal.

Don't overlook soft herbs as salad leaves either: whole leaves of flat-leaf parsley, mint, basil, tarragon, coriander, chives, dill and fennel fronds can totally elevate a green salad. Ready-to-eat bags of salad sold in supermarkets are great when you don't have the time or inclination to make up your own. Just ensure the leaves are as fresh as possible, and always wash them before using.

As always the dressing plays a starring role, but feel free to mix it up and experiment using different dressings from the final chapter.

baby gem and parmesan

This little salad is so tasty you will notice the bowl empty almost as soon as you deliver it to the table. The addition of cheese not only creates a beautifully creamy effect, but also gives substance. To make it more of a main event, add some sundried tomatoes, a few quartered soft-boiled eggs and some Sweet Pickled Red Onions (see page 149).

Serves 4 as a side salad   (V if using Cheddar)

Carbs 2g   Sugar 2g   Protein 6g   Fibre 1g   Fat 5.5g   Sat Fat 3g   Salt 0.2g

50g Parmesan or Cheddar
2 tablespoons natural yogurt
1 teaspoon olive oil
1 teaspoon sherry vinegar
2 baby gem lettuce (about
    350g), roughly torn
salt and freshly ground black
    pepper

Blitz the cheese in a small food-processor until it is nice and crumbly. (This gives a nicer texture than grating it, although in the absence of a food processor this works perfectly.)

In a large bowl, mix three-quarters of the cheese with the yogurt, olive oil, sherry vinegar and a generous pinch of salt and pepper. Pour all over the baby gem leaves and toss to thoroughly coat. Garnish with the remaining cheese and serve.

watercress, rocket and pomegranate

This simple salad is gorgeous with slow-cooked shoulder of lamb
or with hearty stews such as tagines.

Serves 4   calories 95

Carbs 1.5g   Sugar 1.5g   Protein 3g   Fibre 1g   Fat 8.5g   Sat Fat 1g   Salt 0.1g

40g walnuts, roughly chopped
70g watercress
70g wild rocket
2 tablespoons Pomegranate,
   Mint and Coriander
   Dressing (see page 144)

Toast the walnuts in a dry frying pan until golden.
Set aside to cool.

Toss the leaves with the dressing, scatter over the
walnuts and serve.

lemon and lime herb salad

Nothing beats the flavour of a salad bursting with fresh, fragrant,
vibrant herbs. A little avocado is a great addition here.

Serves 4   calories 31

Carbs 1.5g   Sugar 1g   Protein 1g   Fibre 1g   Fat 2g   Sat Fat 0.5g   Salt trace

25g flat-leaf parsley, leaves
   picked
20g basil, leaves picked
15g mint, leaves picked
10g tarragon, leaves picked
100g oak leaf lettuce
2 tablespoons Lemon and Lime
   Vinaigrette (see page 142)
salt and freshly ground black
   pepper

Toss all the leaves with the vinaigrette in a large bowl,
season and serve immediately.

baby leaf and apple with dill, fennel and lemon dressing

This light and crisp salad is a perfect accompaniment to any fish dish.
It goes equally well with meat and poultry. With the addition of some cooked
quinoa, toasted nuts and blue cheese, it becomes a pretty special salad
in its own right.

Serves 4 calories 84   DF GF V VE

Carbs 5.5g   Sugar 5.5g   Protein 1g   Fibre 2g   Fat 6g   Sat Fat 1g   Salt 0.7g

¼ teaspoon fennel seeds
5g dill, fronds roughly chopped,
  plus 5g to garnish
¼ tablespoons caster sugar
½ teaspoon salt
zest of ½ lemon
1 teaspoon wholegrain mustard
2 tablespoons olive oil
1½ tablespoons white wine
  vinegar
170g baby leaves
35g flat-leaf parsley, leaves
  picked
1 pink lady apple, sliced, cored
  and julienned

Grind the fennel seeds, dill, sugar, salt and lemon zest
using a pestle and mortar until you have a paste. Stir in
the wholegrain mustard, followed by the olive oil and
finally the vinegar.

Toss with the leaves, parsley and apple and garnish
with some roughly chopped dill.

comfort salads

Salads are not always known for being comforting, but that doesn't mean they can't be. Wholesome, hearty, filling, satisfying and warming, these are salads that contradict the stereotype. Most belong to winter evenings, eating suppers in front of the fire, maybe with a glass of red for good measure. They give you the best of both worlds — comfort food without the guilt. These are soulful salads, designed to restore and nourish.

After a long day at the office, and a walk home in the rain, the spice hit from the Thai Green Chicken Curry Salad will thaw out those bones. The 'Wind-Me-Down' Winter's Evening Salad will lift the soul. Skinny Pasta Salad and the Pea and Gnocchi Extravaganza will curb those carb cravings and give you a hefty boost of nutrition without weighing you down. The Chargrilled Baby Gem and Egg Ribbons with Spanish Beans will lift any morning fatigue, setting you up for whatever the day ahead holds, while during frosty periods when you are entertaining, Chermoula Scallops with Peas, Broad Beans and Pancetta will impress and satisfy in equal measure.

thai green chicken curry salad

If ever there was a salad that defined comfort, this is it. The curry paste makes a significant amount (350g), but if you are going to go to the trouble, you may as well make loads. Freeze what's left over and use it in dressings, soups, marinades and curries.

Serves 4 calories 275 · DF · GF

Carbs 15g   Sugar 3.5g   Protein 24g   Fibre 4g   Fat 12g   Sat Fat 8.5g   Salt 2.2g

4 skinned and boned chicken
   thighs (about 350g)
150ml coconut milk
50g mix of basmati and wild
   rice
4 heads of baby pak choi (about
   200g), stems removed
200g baby courgettes (or
   1 large), sliced
60g green beans, each sliced
   into three
50g edamame beans (or peas)
2 tablespoons rice vinegar
1 tablespoon fish sauce
salt and freshly ground black
   pepper

Thai green curry paste
70g fresh coconut (available
   prepared in supermarkets)
50g fresh ginger, unpeeled
1 shallot, peeled
2 garlic cloves, peeled
1 lemongrass stalk, roughly
   chopped
1 green bird's eye chilli
60g fresh coriander
1 tablespoon fish sauce
juice of 2 limes

Blitz the ingredients for the paste until smooth. Set aside 100g and freeze the rest.

Place the chicken thighs between two sheets of clingfilm or parchment paper and bash with a rolling pin until really thin.

Mix the curry paste with the coconut milk in a bowl, add the chicken and marinate for a minimum of 30 minutes, or overnight if you are super organised!

Cook the rice according to the packet instructions. When ready, rinse under cold water and set aside to cool, then place in a large bowl with the prepared vegetables.

Remove the chicken from the marinade, scraping off as much of it as possible, and reserve. Heat a chargrill pan until it is smoking hot and cook the chicken thighs for about 4 minutes on each side. You may need to do this in batches. Set aside and keep warm.

Deglaze the pan with the rice vinegar. Pour in the marinade, 100ml water and the fish sauce and simmer for 3–4 minutes. Taste one more time for seasoning, adding a touch more fish sauce or lime juice if necessary.

Pour the hot dressing over the raw vegetables and rice and mix together. Divide between bowls, top with the warm chicken and serve.

winter-warming butternut squash, puy lentils and blue cheese

Most big supermarkets sell ready-cooked pulses such as Puy lentils. I find them great for salads and often have them on hand in my store cupboard to add a little extra substance here and there.

Serves 4

calories 277 · GF · V

Carbs 23g   Sugar 16g   Protein 9g   Fibre 9g   Fat 10.5g   Sat Fat 3.5g   Salt 0.5g

1 butternut squash (about 1–1.5kg)

2 red onions, each sliced into 6 wedges

10 thyme sprigs, leaves picked

2 tablespoons olive oil

2 tablespoons balsamic vinegar

85g cooked Puy lentils

1 quantity Blue Cheese Dressing (see page 48)

100g rocket

1 head of red chicory

salt and freshly ground black pepper

Preheat the oven to 190°C/gas mark 5.

Peel the butternut squash, slice in half, remove and discard the seeds and then cut into wedges about 1cm thick. Place in a large bowl with the red onion and thyme. Pour over the olive oil and balsamic vinegar, add a generous pinch of salt and pepper and toss to thoroughly coat the vegetables.

Divide between two baking trays and roast for 35–40 minutes, turning halfway through and removing any onion wedges that are cooked at this point. When the vegetables are ready, remove from the oven and allow to cool a little.

Microwave the Puy lentils in a bowl covered with clingfilm for a couple of minutes. Transfer the roasted vegetables and lentils to a large bowl and mix these first with the blue cheese dressing, then add the leaves and toss again. Serve immediately. You can also serve this salad cold if you wish.

Tip: This salad would be delicious served with barbecued or grilled steak.

warm lamb kofta salad

This is a salad that no one will want to share, so get in there quick!

Serves 4 calories 287 GF

Carbs 9g   Sugar 7g   Protein 18g   Fibre 2g   Fat 19g   Sat Fat 6.5g   Salt 0.2g

For the lamb kofta

325g lamb shoulder or neck
   fillet, minced
4 thyme sprigs, leaves picked
zest of ½ lemon
I garlic clove, finely grated
   or chopped
I teaspoon sumac powder
¼ teaspoon mild chilli powder
¼ teaspoon ground cumin
¼ teaspoon ground coriander
¾ teaspoon pomegranate
   molasses
generous pinch of salt and
   freshly ground black pepper
2 tablespoons olive oil

For the salad

80g mixed leaves
40g flat-leaf parsley, leaves
   picked
40g mint, leaves picked
juice of ½ lemon
I quantity Sumac, Chilli and
   Lemon Yogurt Dressing (see
   page 145)
¼ jar of Sweet Pickled Red
   Onions (see page 149), or
   I small red onion, sliced into
   rings and mixed with juice of
   ½ lemon

Soak 4 wooden skewers in water for 20 minutes. In
a medium bowl, mix the kofta ingredients together,
except the oil, so that the flavours are evenly distributed.

Divide the mixture into four, and mould onto skewers
in a long, thin sausage-like shape. This step can be
done in advance. Refrigerate for 30 minutes before
cooking to allow the meat to firm up.

When ready, coat a griddle or frying pan with the olive
oil and place over a high heat. When very hot, add the
skewers and cook for about 8 minutes, turning so that
all sides get nicely browned. Allow the koftas to rest
while you prepare the rest of the salad.

Toss the mixed leaves, parsley and mint with the lemon
juice, I tablespoon of the dressing and a generous
pinch of salt and pepper. Serve with the koftas, pickled
red onions and the remaining dressing in a bowl for
everyone to drizzle over their salad.

Tips: If you are in an organised mood, like I am every
now and again, make double or triple the kofta mixture
and freeze it. These kofta are a great standby to have in
your freezer, especially in summer months, when they
are amazing on the barbecue!

Rosemary stalks make for great skewers – simply remove
all of the leaves except for those at the top.

spinach, fig and buckwheat with walnut-crusted pork

Pork tenderloin is a seriously underused piece of meat: it's affordable, quick to cook and, when treated properly, totally delicious. Here it feels decadent, and deserving of its pride of place.

Serves 4

Carbs 24.5g   Sugar 12g   Protein 20g   Fibre 3g   Fat 12g   Sat Fat 2g   Salt 0.3g

40g walnuts
½ tablespoon agave nectar
1½ teaspoons five-spice powder
275g pork tenderloin
60g raw buckwheat
200g baby spinach
1½ tablespoons fresh thyme
   leaves
½ tablespoon olive oil
3 dried figs, diced
6 Pickled Smoked Cherry
   Tomatoes (see page 155,
   optional), halved
2 tablespoons balsamic vinegar
juice of ½ lemon
salt and freshly ground black
   pepper

Using a pestle and mortar, grind the walnuts with the agave nectar and five-spice powder until you have a rough paste. Add 2 tablespoons of hot water and a pinch of salt and pepper and stir.

Slice the pork tenderloin in half lengthways, place between two sheets of clingfilm or parchment paper and bash with a wooden rolling pin until it is as flat as it will go. Slice into very thin strips and add to the walnut paste. Marinate for at least 30 minutes, or overnight if possible.

Cook the buckwheat according to the packet instructions. Tip into a sieve and drain and rinse under cold water to cool.

When you are ready to make the salad, mix the cooled buckwheat with the spinach and thyme in a large bowl.

Place a large frying pan over a very high heat. Add the olive oil and, when smoking hot, fry the pork strips for about 5 minutes, or until nicely browned and cooked through. Transfer immediately to the bowl with the spinach and buckwheat.

Put the frying pan back over a medium heat and add the figs, tomatoes, balsamic vinegar and lemon juice. Reduce a little then pour over the salad and mix to combine. Season with a generous pinch of salt and pepper and serve immediately.

chargrilled baby gem and egg ribbons with spanish beans

I wanted to write a recipe for a breakfast salad of sorts and this is my idea of a perfect start to the day, although I could eat this for breakfast, lunch and dinner. If making egg ribbons feels like more effort than you are willing to dedicate to this recipe, try scrambling them, or soft boil for 6 minutes.

Serves 4 calories 264 DF

Carbs 18g   Sugar 7g   Protein 15g   Fibre 8g   Fat 13g   Sat Fat 4g   Salt 0.9g

2 medium free-range eggs
1 tablespoon olive oil
2 baby gem lettuce, each cut into 4 wedges
salt and freshly ground black pepper

For the Spanish beans
50g spicy cooking chorizo, finely chopped
50g morcilla (or black pudding)
250g cherry or baby plum tomatoes
400g can tomatoes
400g can haricot/cannellini beans
1 teaspoon smoked paprika
3 or 4 thyme sprigs, leaves picked
80g spinach, finely shredded
1 tablespoon red wine vinegar

First make the beans. Fry the chorizo and morcilla (or black pudding) in a dry frying pan over a medium heat for about 5 minutes until crispy. Add the fresh and canned tomatoes, beans, paprika and thyme, stir well and simmer for 20–25 minutes. Stir in the spinach and red wine vinegar. Season to taste.

Whisk the eggs with 1 tablespoon of water. Brush a medium non-stick frying pan with a little oil and place over a medium heat. Pour in a quarter of the egg mixture and swirl all around the pan so that it is fully coated – it will be very thin. After a minute or two, flip and cook for 30 seconds on the other side. Remove and set aside while you cook three more pancakes, then leave the pan over the heat for the baby gem. When ready, roll into a log shape and slice into long strips or ribbons.

Drizzle the baby gem with the remaining olive oil and season with salt and pepper. Char for a couple of minutes on each side until nicely browned. Serve a nice spoonful of beans with the baby gem topped with the egg ribbons. Heaven!

protein salad with a punch

This is a high-impact protein salad that is amazingly low in calories considering how substantial it is. If you can't find gochujang, instead use chilli sauce, such as Sriracha, but bear in mind it will be significantly spicier.

Serves 4   calories 299 DF

Carbs 16.5g   Sugar 4g   Protein 25g   Fibre 4.5g   Fat 14g   Sat Fat 3.5g   Salt 2g

150g lean minced beef
2 tablespoons soy sauce or tamari
1 teaspoon sesame oil
½ tablespoon sesame seeds
60g brown rice vermicelli noodles
1 head of pak choi (about 150g), finely sliced
4 pink radishes, finely sliced
1 fennel bulb (about 250g), finely sliced
100g edamame beans, soaked in boiling water for 2 minutes then drained
20g coriander, leaves picked
1 tablespoon olive oil
4 medium free-range eggs
salt and freshly ground black pepper

For the dressing
100g silken tofu
2 tablespoons gochujang (Korean chilli paste)
1 teaspoon fish sauce
juice of 1 lime

First make the dressing. Blitz all the ingredients with a hand-held blender until smooth.

Mix the beef with 1 tablespoon of the soy sauce and the sesame oil and seeds and season with salt and pepper. Fry in a dry non-stick frying pan over a high heat until browned and crispy, about 10–15 minutes. Set aside.

Cover the rice noodles with boiling water from the kettle, leave for about 5 minutes, then drain and run under cool water. Dress with the remaining tablespoon of soy sauce.

Arrange the noodles, pak choi, radishes, fennel, edamame beans and coriander in four big bowls and pour the dressing on top.

Clean and return the frying pan to the heat and add the olive oil. Crack the eggs into the pan, cover loosely with a large lid or baking tray, and when the whites are thoroughly cooked and the yolk just set (about 4–5 minutes), remove and place on top of the salad. Serve immediately.

pea and gnocchi extravaganza

I need carbs in my life: there are hungers that nothing else will cure or satisfy. This salad is filling without being overly heavy. Expect your carb cravings to be quelled and your energy levels boosted — all without leaving you feeling weighed down, bloated or sluggish.

Serves 4 calories 265 V

Carbs 35g   Sugar 4.5g   Protein 8.5g   Fibre 5.5g   Fat 9g   Sat Fat 1g   Salt 0.9g

350g gnocchi
150g frozen peas
100g sugarsnap peas, halved
  lengthways
100g mangetout, sliced
70g pea shoots

For the dressing
1 small shallot, roughly
  chopped
2 tablespoons olive oil
1 tablespoon red wine vinegar
15g mint, leaves picked
15g basil, leaves picked
juice of 1½ lemons and zest
  of ½
1 tablespoon pine nuts
salt and freshly ground black
  pepper

Cook the gnocchi according to the packet instructions then drain and refresh under cold water.

Cover the peas with boiling water from the kettle, leave for a couple of minutes then drain and refresh as above.

Put all the ingredients for the dressing into a blender and blitz until smooth. Season to taste. Let out with a dash of water if the dressing is a little thick.

Put the gnocchi, peas, sugarsnap peas, mangetout and pea shoots into a big bowl, pour over the dressing and toss so all the ingredients are thoroughly coated. Taste once more for seasoning, adjust if necessary and serve.

Tips: If you are a chilli fan, add ¼ teaspoon of chilli flakes to the dressing for a lovely spicy counterbalance to the sweet peas.

You can buy gluten-free gnocchi, but if you can't find it use gluten-free pasta to make this recipe suitable for a gluten-free diet.

a 'wind-me-down' winter's evening salad

This salad is great for a winter's evening when you feel a bit beaten down by your day. It is the kind of food that helps you unwind and relax, and it would be delicious enjoyed with a nice glass of smooth, mellow, fruity red wine — although that would tip this salad over the 300-calorie mark!

Serves 4

Carbs 17g   Sugar 7.5g   Protein 13g   Fibre 11.5g   Fat 15g   Sat Fat 3g   Salt 0.7g

400g purple sprouting
   broccoli
400g can chickpeas, drained
250g kale
1½ tablespoons olive oil
2 tablespoons balsamic vinegar
80g Homemade Ricotta (see
   page 151), to garnish
salt and freshly ground black
   pepper

For the dressing
2 tablespoons wholegrain
   mustard
2 tablespoons balsamic vinegar
½ tablespoon olive oil
juice of ½ lemon
8 Kalamata olives, pitted

Preheat the oven to 200°C/gas mark 6.

Put the purple sprouting broccoli and chickpeas in a large bowl and the kale in another. Season generously. Dress the broccoli and chickpeas with the olive oil and the kale with balsamic vinegar. Ensure everything is thoroughly coated.

Spread the broccoli and chickpeas onto a large baking tray and roast for 10 minutes.

To roast the kale, you may need to work in batches. Spread it in a single layer on a large baking tray and roast for 5 minutes. This is long enough for the edges to crisp slightly and for the kale to soften.

Blend all the dressing ingredients together using a hand-held stick blender or mini food-processor.

Allow the vegetables to cool a little, then transfer them to a large bowl. Dress while still warm and serve straight away, garnished with the ricotta.

Tip: Shop-bought ricotta will also work here, as will feta cheese.

bacon and egg salad

This salad is traditionally named a Lyonnaise Salad, but I think any dish adorned with bacon and eggs needs to scream it from the rooftops! Thank you to Polly for the inspiration for this recipe.

Serves 4 calories 278 DF

Carbs 12.5g Sugar 2g Protein 15g Fibre 1.5g Fat 18g Sat Fat 5g Salt 1.6g

90g thinly sliced pancetta
1 small shallot, finely diced
2 tablespoons red wine vinegar
1 teaspoon Dijon mustard
1–2 tablespoons olive oil
white wine vinegar
4 medium free-range eggs
200g frisée lettuce
100g day-old sourdough bread, roughly torn into small chunks
salt and freshly ground black pepper

Quickly fry the strips of pancetta in a dry, non-stick frying pan until crisp. You may need to do this in batches. Remove from the pan and drain on a piece of kitchen paper. Add the shallot to the pan and sauté in the residual fat until soft. Add the red wine vinegar and mustard and stir. Add 1 tablespoon of olive oil, plus an extra tablespoon if there isn't enough fat from the bacon to create a dressing. Season with salt and pepper and remove from the heat.

Fill a saucepan with water, add a splash of white wine vinegar and bring to a gentle simmer. Have a bowl of ice-cold water on standby. Cook the eggs one at a time. Break an egg into a small cup or bowl, gently stir the water in the pan so that it is swirling, drop the egg into the centre and poach for 3 minutes. Remove using a slotted spoon and place in the bowl of cold water while you cook the rest.

When ready to serve, place the frisée and bread in a large bowl and crumble over the pancetta. Heat the dressing, pour all over and toss. Plunge the eggs into a saucepan or big bowl of very hot water to reheat and serve on top of the salad.

Tip: For a (72 calories per portion) lighter salad, omit the bread.

skinny pasta salad

Sometimes, there is only one remedy for my hunger, and that is a bowl of pasta. If I am tired, run down or a bit fed up, I want what I eat to make me feel better. This pasta salad fills those hunger gaps, cheers up a crappy day and even makes me feel better about everything. Food should feed your soul, as well as your belly – this does both.

Serves 4   calories 269   DF   V

Carbs 36g   Sugar 5g   Protein 11g   Fibre 5g   Fat 8g   Sat Fat 3g   Salt 1g

175g pasta, e.g. casarecce or penne
1 green courgette, diced
1 yellow courgette, diced
50g radish sprouts, or whatever sprouts you can find or grow (optional, see page 13)
60g Kalamata olives, pitted
5g chives, finely chopped
65g feta cheese, crumbled
15 Pickled Smoked Cherry Tomatoes, quartered (see page 155)
60g Roasted Red Pepper, Basil and Chilli Dressing (see page 145)
salt

Cook the pasta according to the packet instructions in well-salted water. Tip into a sieve, drain and rinse under cold water to cool.

Transfer to a bowl, add all the remaining ingredients and mix thoroughly. Season to taste and serve.

Tips: Use a few sundried tomatoes if you don't have smoked pickled tomatoes. To make this gluten-free, use gluten-free pasta. Chermoula (see page 144) would be a great dressing here, too.

chermoula scallops with peas, broad beans and pancetta

My love of scallops is very much inspired by my Mum; they are her all time favourite. This dish is sophisticated and elegant, just like her, and is exactly how I imagine she would love eating them. Crispy pancetta is an indulgent addition and, if you really want to show off, serve the scallops in their shells.

Serves 4 calories 290 DF GF

Carbs 15g · Sugar 6g · Protein 25g · Fibre 11.5g · Fat 12g · Sat Fat 2.5g · Salt 1g

300g frozen peas
350g frozen broad beans
12 medium scallops
100ml Chermoula Dressing
 (see page 144)
4 thin slices pancetta
1½ tablespoons olive oil
1 lemon, sliced into 4 wedges
salt and freshly ground black
 pepper

Preheat the oven to 200°C/gas mark 6. Line a baking tray with parchment paper.

Put the peas and broad beans into separate bowls, cover with boiling water from the kettle and leave for 5 minutes. Drain and refresh under cold water. Pop the broad beans out of their skins. Set aside until needed.

Put the scallops in a bowl and toss with 1 tablespoon of the dressing, then place on the lined baking tray, along with the slices of pancetta. Place in the oven and after 8 minutes, remove the scallops. If the pancetta is not yet crispy, give it another few minutes.

To serve, arrange the peas and broad beans on a large serving platter. Place the scallops on top, along with generous spoonfuls of chermoula dressing. Crumble the crispy pancetta all over and finish with a drizzle of olive oil and a sprinkle of salt and pepper. Serve with the lemon wedges.

aromatic prawn and coconut steamed parcel

Try to find parchment paper that is 40cm wide for this recipe. This longer width will mean you can create a pouch with a single sheet. Aluminium foil will also work well.

Serves 4 calories 168 DF GF

Carbs 5.5g   Sugar 4g   Protein 16g   Fibre 2g   Fat 8g   Sat Fat 6.5g   Salt 1.4g

240g beansprouts
150g cucumber, deseeded and sliced into thin matchsticks
3 spring onions, julienned
300g fresh raw prawns, shelled
25g coriander, leaves picked
pinch of freshly ground black pepper

For the dressing
170ml coconut milk
1½ tablespoons rice vinegar
1 tablespoon fish sauce
2 red bird's eye chillies, halved
20g fresh ginger, peeled and roughly sliced
1 lemongrass stalk, bruised
1 shallot, roughly chopped
3 kaffir lime leaves (optional)
2 garlic cloves

Preheat the oven to 200°C/gas mark 6.

Start by preparing the dressing. Put all the ingredients in a saucepan with 100ml water, bring to the boil and simmer until reduced by half, about 15 minutes. Strain and set aside.

Mix the beansprouts, cucumber and spring onion together in a large bowl. Cut four squares of parchment paper, about 40cm long, and lay them out on a flat surface. Divide the beansprout mixture and prawns between each piece of parchment and pour over the dressing.

Gather all four corners of the paper together so you create a small pouch encasing the ingredients and seal by twisting the paper tightly together. Transfer to a baking tray and cook for 15 minutes. Serve immediately, topped with the coriander leaves and a pinch of freshly ground black pepper.

simple salads

Salads are often among the simplest of dishes to make, but the collection of recipes in this chapter are particularly straightforward. A salad as undemanding as Avocado, Tomato and Pomegranate is a must for any salad-lover's repertoire, requiring minimum effort but delivering maximum impact. Roasted Red Pepper and Chicory with Caper Berries and Salami is my go-to salad when I am entertaining and need something truly special but unapologetically simple to make. Squid and Tomato with Lime and Pepper Dressing is a flavour sensation, and a recipe even the most unconfident of cooks could master. If you are a sushi lover, the Hawaiian Tuna Poke (*poh-kay*) is an absolute must. Be sure to ask for sushi-grade fish from your fishmonger. This essentially translates as the best-quality fish they have, which is suitable to eat raw. Simple recipes can be as (or sometimes more) spectacular as the most complicated ones, and the ones in this chapter are guaranteed to give you a feel-good factor when you're preparing them.

grilled aubergine with red butterhead and salsa verde

It takes a little while for the aubergines to char, even over a high heat, but be patient and persevere – the flavour you get from a chargilled aubergine is quite unlike any other.

Serves 4

Carbs 7g   Sugar 6g   Protein 3g   Fibre 8g   Fat 7g   Sat Fat 1g   Salt 0.4g

3 large aubergines, a mixture of different varieties if you can find them
1 tablespoon olive oil
½ red (or green) butterhead lettuce
3 tablespoons Salsa Verde Dressing (see page 143)
salt and freshly ground black pepper

Slice each aubergine into four lengthways. Use a pastry brush to brush the aubergine slices on each side with a little olive oil, then season generously with salt and pepper.

Place a griddle pan over a high heat and, when smoking hot, add the aubergines. (You will need to cook them in batches.) Cook on each side until beautifully charred – don't be tempted to turn them over before they have taken on plenty of colour. Set the cooked aubergine aside and keep warm.

Place three or four butterhead leaves on each plate, top with the chargrilled aubergine and serve with the salsa verde.

chilled cucumber with lemon and lime dressing

This salad is at its best when served chilled. It is a delicious accompaniment to seared tuna or ceviche but even on its own, it will make your taste buds dance.

Serves 4

Carbs 2.5g Sugar 2.5g Protein 2g Fibre 1.5g Fat 4g Sat Fat 0.5g Salt trace

2 chilled cucumbers
3 tablespoons Lemon and Lime
  Vinaigrette (see page 142),
  chilled
a few small mint leaves
salt

Peel the cucumbers and slice into rounds about 1cm thick. Toss with the dressing and serve with a sprinkle of salt and a few little mint leaves.

Tip: This salad is delicious served with some sea bass ceviche. Thinly slice 2 skinned fillets of best-quality fresh sea bass. Marinade for 5 minutes in the juice of 2 lemons, then add a generous pinch of chilli flakes and salt.

miso mushrooms with iceberg

This recipe is inspired by two restaurants I love, one serves iceberg with a miso dressing and little else, and the other, mushrooms with miso and eggs for breakfast. I love both dishes equally and they have inspired me to create this recipe. I debated whether to feature it in this chapter because the list of ingredients is slightly longer and some of them are more unusual, but it is just so ridiculously easy to make, it couldn't go anywhere else!

Serves 4

Carbs 4g   Sugar 2g   Protein 4.5g   Fibre 1g   Fat 4g   Sat Fat 0.5g   Salt 1.4g

350g mixed exotic mushrooms,
  e.g. enoki and king oyster
1 iceberg lettuce
5g flat-leaf parsley, finely
  chopped
1 small red chilli, finely sliced
1 tablespoon toasted sesame
  seeds
1 lime, cut into 4 wedges

For the dressing

2 tablespoons sweet white miso
1 tablespoon light soy sauce or
  tamari
¾ tablespoon rice wine vinegar
1 teaspoon mirin (or use a
  pinch of sugar)
1 teaspoon sesame oil (use
  toasted for a more robust
  flavour)
10g fresh ginger, peeled and
  finely grated
¼ teaspoon chilli flakes (use
  more or less depending on
  your spice preference)

Preheat the grill to its highest setting.

To make the dressing, mix all the ingredients together with 1½ tablespoons water until smooth.

Toss the mushrooms in 2 tablespoons of the dressing. Grill for 3–4 minutes, keeping a very close eye on them to ensure they are not burning. Turn them over when they are nicely browned on one side. You may need to cook the mushrooms in batches – what is most important is to ensure they cook in an even layer rather than pile them all on at once.

Meanwhile, remove the outer leaves of the iceberg and trim the root. Cut into 4 wedges.

Place the iceberg on a plate and pour over half the dressing. Top with the mushrooms, parsley, chilli and sesame seeds. Cover with the rest of the dressing and serve with lime wedges.

avocado, tomato and pomegranate

Creamy avocado, juicy tomatoes, crunchy pomegranate seeds:
the ingredients within this salad do all the work — the only dressing needed
is a drop of great olive oil and a squeeze of lemon juice to bring it all
together. A salad this easy, this delicious and so visually beautiful should
be on all of our repertoires.

Serves 4

Carbs 16g   Sugar 14g   Protein 4.5g   Fibre 9g   Fat 21g   Sat Fat 4g   Salt trace

600g cherry tomatoes
(use mixed varieties if you
can find them)
1 large or 2 small pomegranates
(about 300g)
2 ripe avocados
1 lemon
2 tablespoons extra virgin
olive oil
60g basil, leaves picked
(or Greek basil, if you can
find it)
salt and freshly ground black
pepper

Cut the tomatoes into quarters, or halves if you don't
have the patience. Slice the pomegranate(s) in half,
then tear into quarters and gently remove the seeds by
hand. Or you can bash the top of each pomegranate
half with a wooden spoon to release the seeds into a
bowl, but this splashes pomegranate juice everywhere,
so I opt for the calmer approach!

Peel and stone the avocados and roughly dice the flesh.
Slice the lemon in half and squeeze the juice from one
half over the diced avocado.

Put the tomatoes, pomegranate seeds and avocado into
a large bowl and gently fold in the olive oil and the
juice from the remaining lemon half. Season to taste.
Serve garnished with freshly torn basil.

Tip: You can often buy pomegranate seeds ready
prepared in supermarkets, if you don't want to buy
them whole and remove the seeds yourself.

tomato with mustard-seed and curry-leaf dressing

I love this salad because it can be concocted mainly from ingredients in your store cupboard, and it turns even watery and somewhat insipid tomatoes into something quite special. Fresh curry leaves can be difficult to come by, but dried ones are sold in most big supermarkets and will work here, too. I like this salad on its own, but it is also an amazing accompaniment to a curry.

Serves 4 calories 84 DF GF V VE

Carbs 5g   Sugar 5g   Protein 2.5g   Fibre 2g   Fat 6g   Sat Fat 1g   Salt 0g

1½ tablespoons groundnut oil
1 garlic clove, finely sliced
1 cinnamon stick
3 teaspoons black mustard seeds
1½ teaspoons cumin seeds
3 dried bird's eye chillies
about 35 fresh curry leaves
juice of ½ lime
600g ripe plum tomatoes, sliced
lime wedges, to serve
salt and freshly ground black pepper

Gently heat the oil in a frying pan and add the garlic. Allow it to simmer until it just starts to turn golden brown, then remove using a slotted spoon, being careful not to burn yourself.

Add the cinnamon stick, mustard and cumin seeds, chillies and curry leaves and simmer for a minute or so until the seeds begin to pop. Remove from the heat and allow to settle and cool a little bit before adding the lime juice. Season with a pinch of salt and pepper and set aside to cool.

When ready to serve, remove the cinnamon stick and whole dried chillies from the dressing and pour all over the tomatoes. Gently toss to dress. The juice released from the tomatoes will further enhance the dressing, so toss well. Serve with lime wedges.

Tip: If using dried curry leaves, reduce the quantity to 15; the flavour of dried is slightly different to fresh and using too many leaves can be overpowering.

squid and tomato with lime and pepper dressing

I ate a dish similar to this while travelling the south coast of Cambodia and remember thinking the flavour combination of squid, pepper and lime was one of the most sublime I had ever tasted. Best-quality squid will make this salad as good as it should be, so it's well worth a trip to your fishmonger.

Serves 4 calories 144 DF GF

Carbs 3g Sugar 3g Protein 23g Fibre 1g Fat 4g Sat Fat 1g Salt 0.4g

4 small squid, washed, cleaned and prepared (ask your fishmonger to do this)
1 teaspoon olive oil
350g tomatoes (heirloom, beef or plum), sliced
a few dill sprigs, to garnish
salt

For the dressing
2 teaspoons peppercorns
juice of 1 lime
1 teaspoon extra virgin olive oil

Slice down the side of each squid and open out flat. Dry with kitchen paper then, using a very sharp knife, score the flesh on the inside in a crisscross pattern, making sure you don't cut right through. (If you score the surface of the flesh, it won't curl up when you cook it). Cut each squid into six to eight pieces, depending on its size. Coat both the scored squid pieces and the tentacles with the olive oil and a generous pinch of salt.

To make the dressing, grind the peppercorns using a pestle and mortar until you have a coarse powder. Add the lime juice and olive oil and mix well. Transfer to a large bowl.

Heat a griddle pan until smoking hot (you could also use a barbecue for this). Cook the squid for 1–2 minutes on each side, but no more.

Add the cooked squid to the dressing, leave to cool a little, then add the tomatoes. Serve immediately, garnished with dill.

carrot and celeriac
with brown shrimp

You can buy brown shrimp from lots of big supermarkets and fishmongers. They are wonderfully punchy in flavour and adorn this salad beautifully, turning two everyday ingredients into something really special.

Serves 4 calories 85 GF

Carbs 6g   Sugar 5g   Protein 7g   Fibre 7g   Fat 2g   Sat Fat 1g   Salt 0.7g

For the dressing
2½ tablespoons natural yogurt
2½ tablespoons Greek-style yogurt
¾ teaspoon grated horseradish (fresh or from a jar)
small bunch of dill, fronds roughly torn
3 heaped teaspoons capers, roughly chopped
zest and juice of ½ lemon
salt and freshly ground black pepper

For the salad
1 large carrot (approx. 150g)
1 small celeriac (approx. 450g)
100g cooked brown shrimp

To garnish
small bunch of dill
Tabasco sauce (optional)

First make the dressing. Mix all the ingredients together, leave for about 10 minutes for the flavours to develop, then season to taste.

Peel the carrot and celeriac. Use a potato peeler to create long thin ribbons of each. Alternatively, the grater attachment of your food-processor will do the job.

In a bowl, mix the carrot and celeriac ribbons with half the brown shrimp. Add the dressing and gently toss together.

Serve garnished with the remaining brown shrimp, some roughly torn dill and a drizzle of Tabasco sauce, if using.

Hawaiian tuna poke

Poke (pronounced *poh-kay*) is a traditional Hawaiian dish made using Japanese ingredients. It is often a grab-and-go affair and different versions of it can be found all over the island. Traditionally, it is made from fresh raw tuna marinated in soy sauce, sesame oil and onions, served with sushi rice seasoned with seaweed, Hawaiian salt, and local candlenuts (similar to macadamia nuts). But if you have great tuna and nicely seasoned rice, the rest is up to you. This is my version, and I hope you love it as much as I do!

Serves 4 calories 296 DF

Carbs 26.5g   Sugar 4g   Protein 28g   Fibre 2.5g   Fat 8g   Sat Fat 1.5g   Salt 1.2g

320g sushi-grade tuna, cut into 1cm cubes

3 tablespoons soy sauce or tamari, plus extra to drizzle

¾ tablespoon sesame oil

10g fresh ginger, peeled and finely grated

100g sushi rice

1 tablespoon rice wine vinegar

120g edamame beans

80g silken tofu

2 tablespoons sriracha

juice of ½ lime

1 tablespoon sesame seeds

½ avocado, peeled and finely sliced

3 radishes, julienned

a few coriander sprigs, leaves picked and finely chopped

To garnish

shichimi togarashi spice mix (optional)

lime wedges

Toss the tuna with the soy sauce, sesame oil and grated ginger. Cover with clingfilm and refrigerate.

Cook the rice in salted water according to the packet instructions. When ready, stir in the rice wine vinegar and allow to cool completely.

Put the edamame beans in a bowl, cover with boiling water from the kettle and leave for 2–3 minutes, then drain and refresh in cold water. Stir through the rice.

Blitz the tofu with the sriracha and lime juice until completely smooth. Toast the sesame seeds in a dry frying pan until golden.

Serve the rice topped with the marinated tuna, avocado, radishes, coriander, sriracha sauce and sesame seeds. Garnish with shichimi togarashi (if using) and a squeeze of lime juice.

Tip: If you can't find shichimi togarashi, just season with salt and pepper instead.

roasted red pepper and chicory with caper berries and salami

This recipe is a simple collection of delicious ingredients. I used a fennel and pepper salami, bought from my local deli, where they slice it there and then (supermarket delis will provide this service too). You could use pickled roasted red peppers (see page 154 or use shop-bought) in place of the romano peppers; they are useful to keep in your store cupboard.

Serves 4

Carbs 9.5g Sugar 6.5g Protein 4g Fibre 4.5g Fat 7.5g Sat Fat 2.5g Salt 0.4g

3 romano peppers, quartered
  lengthways and deseeded
4 thyme sprigs, leaves picked
2 rosemary sprigs, leaves picked
1 tablespoon olive oil
1 teaspoon agave nectar
  (or agave nectar from toasted
  hazelnuts, see page 148)
1 tablespoon sherry vinegar
10g flat-leaf parsley leaves
  finely chopped
2 heads of red chicory, leaves
  separated
8 wafer-thin slices salami
15 caper berries
salt and freshly ground black
  pepper

Preheat the oven to 200°C/gas mark 6.

Lay the peppers flat in a deep baking tray, scatter over the thyme and rosemary, season with salt and pepper, drizzle with olive oil and roast for 30 minutes.

Transfer the peppers to a large bowl, reserving as much of the roasting oil and juice from the peppers as possible. To make the dressing, stir the agave nectar, sherry vinegar and parsley into the reserved roasting juices and season to taste.

Add the chicory leaves to the roasted peppers and gently mix together. Transfer to a large serving platter, along with the salami and caper berries. Drizzle the dressing all over and serve.

summer on a plate

In the world we live in, you can have summer on a plate any time of the year — these ingredients are easy to buy all the time. However, if you are shopping seasonally and have access to fresh broad beans in their pods, do use them. That said, frozen broad beans are also great, and will work perfectly in this salad if you can't find fresh ones.

Serves 4

Carbs 15.5g   Sugar 10g   Protein 8.5g   Fibre 10.5g   Fat 3g   Sat Fat 0.6g   Salt 0.2g

300g baby carrots, peeled and halved lengthways
350g podded broad beans (about 1.25–1.5kg unpodded)
1 quantity Sumac, Chilli and Lemon Yogurt Dressing (see page 145)
170g sugarsnap peas, halved lengthways
150g radishes, halved

To garnish
2–3 mint sprigs, leaves picked and finely shredded
lemon wedges
sumac powder (optional)
salt and freshly ground black pepper

Put the carrots in a medium saucepan with a generous pinch of salt, cover with water, bring to the boil and simmer for 3–4 minutes. Drain and refresh under cold water. Set aside until needed.

Cover the broad beans with boiling water. Drain after 2–3 minutes if using fresh, and 3–4 minutes if using frozen. Refresh under cold water. Remove the outer skin of each broad bean to release the vibrant bean from inside — this takes a little time but is worth it!

To serve, generously spread a big spoonful of the dressing across a plate. Arrange the vegetables on top and garnish with mint and some wedges of lemon to squeeze over. Sprinkle over some sumac (if using) and salt and pepper and serve the remaining dressing in a little jar for people to use more if they wish.

roasted vegetables and giant couscous

This is a crowd-pleaser kind of salad, and one I often rustle up when entertaining. You are not tied to using giant couscous; use whatever grains you favour or have to hand. Don't be tempted to load the veggies onto one tray — they will sweat and steam rather than roast — separate them between two, and spread in a single layer. (If your trays are on the smaller side, you may need to cook the vegetables in two batches.) The salsa verde dressing works beautifully here, serving to cut through the sweetness of the vegetables.

Serves 4

calories 255   DF

....

Carbs 28g   Sugar 8.5g   Protein 7g   Fibre 7g   Fat 11g   Sat Fat 2g   Salt 0.8g

....

1 medium aubergine
2 medium courgettes
2 peppers, a mixture of red,
  orange or yellow
1 red onion, finely sliced
2 rosemary sprigs, leaves picked
5 thyme sprigs, leaves picked
3 tablespoons olive oil
1 vegetable or chicken stock
  cube
100g giant couscous
1½ tablespoons Salsa Verde
  Dressing (see page 143)
5g flat-leaf parsley leaves, finely
  chopped, to garnish
salt and freshly ground black
  pepper

Preheat the oven to 200°C/gas mark 6. Line two large baking trays with foil and set aside.

Chop the aubergines, courgettes and peppers. I like to chop them quite small (roughly 1cm dice), but go bigger if you prefer. Put the vegetables in a large bowl, along with the sliced red onion, herbs and a generous pinch of salt and pepper. Add the olive oil and use your hands to gently toss the vegetables, ensuring they are thoroughly coated. Spread in an even layer on the baking trays and roast for 20–25 minutes.

Meanwhile, bring a pan of water to the boil along with the stock cube. Add the couscous and cook for 10–12 minutes, until al dente. Drain under cold water and set aside.

When the vegetables are roasted, allow to cool slightly, then mix with the couscous. Dress with the salsa verde, garnish with chopped parsley and serve.

Tip: A few pickled smoked cherry tomatoes (see page 155) would be a lovely addition to this salad.

cavolo nero, spring onions and sweetcorn with chermoula

Chargrilling these vegetables transforms them completely — especially the spring onions. If you were to eat this salad with the components raw, it would be unrecognisable. So addictive are the flavours, you could say it's not for sharing!

Serves 4

Carbs 9g   Sugar 6.5g   Protein 5g   Fibre 5g   Fat 8.3g   Sat Fat 1g   Salt 0.4g

200g spring onions, trimmed and halved lengthways
400g cavolo nero, tough inner stalks removed
2 fresh corn on the cob (about 450g)
2 tablespoons olive oil
2 tablespoons Chermoula Dressing (see page 144)
salt and freshly ground black pepper

Coat the vegetables with the olive oil and season with salt and pepper. Place a griddle pan over a high heat and, when smoking hot, grill the spring onions and cavolo nero until lightly charred and wilted. Remove and set aside.

Now grill the sweetcorn until slightly blackened on all sides. When ready, leave to cool a little before slicing the kernels from the cob.

Toss everything with the dressing and serve.

Tip: Some shredded chicken would be great with this salad.

chilli-roasted sweet potato, cauliflower, rocket and ricotta

This salad shows just how a dressing can transfer simple ingredients into something really special — and beautiful. This one is a real crowd pleaser. Perfect for parties!

Serves 4   calories 286 GF V

Carbs 27g   Sugar 15g   Protein 8g   Fibre 7.5g   Fat 14g   Sat Fat 3g   Salt 0.7g

I sweet potato (about 250g), cut into 3cm cubes
I medium cauliflower (about 750g), broken into florets
2 teaspoons chilli flakes
5 thyme sprigs, leaves picked
2 tablespoons olive oil
100g rocket
I quantity Pomegranate, Mint and Coriander Dressing (see page 144)
50g Homemade Ricotta (see page 151) or feta cheese, crumbled
salt and freshly ground black pepper

Preheat the oven to 200°C/gas mark 6. Line a large baking tray with foil.

Toss the sweet potato and cauliflower with the chilli flakes, thyme and olive oil. Spread in an even layer on the baking tray, season generously and roast for 20 minutes.

When cool, toss with the rocket and half of the dressing and finish with the ricotta or feta cheese. Serve the remaining dressing for people to help themselves to more if they wish.

balsamic-roasted radish and mozzarella

This salad uses radishes and their leafy tops, which you can often find in good greengrocers. Ensure you buy bunches with fresh vibrant leaves and wash them really well to remove any grit. If you can't find them like this, 100g of lamb's lettuce or curly lollo rosso would make a great alternative.

Serves 4

Carbs 14g   Sugar 14.5g   Protein 8g   Fibre 1g   Fat 11.5g   Sat Fat 4g   Salt 0.4g

2 big bunches of radishes with leaves attached (about 900g–1kg)
3 tablespoons balsamic vinegar
1 tablespoon agave nectar or honey
1 tablespoon olive oil
small bunch of thyme, leaves picked and finely chopped
1 teaspoon sumac powder
100g mozzarella
50g pomegranate seeds
30g pistachios, roughly chopped
salt and freshly ground black pepper

Preheat the oven to 180°C/gas mark 4.

Separate the leaves from the radishes and wash and dry both thoroughly. You will need 100g of leaves.

Mix together the balsamic vinegar, agave nectar or honey, olive oil, thyme, sumac, salt and pepper. Place the radishes on a baking tray, pour the dressing over and roast for 20 minutes. When ready, remove from the oven and set aside to cool.

Put the radish leaves in a large bowl, scatter over the roasted radishes and pour over the dressing from the baking tray. Toss and then tear over the mozzarella. Finish with the pomegranate seeds and pistachios.

classic salads

The reason recipes such as these stand the test of time is because they are, quite simply, perfectly blissful collections of flavours, seamlessly and beautifully balanced.

Many, such as Panzanella and Greek Salad, are truly classic, whereas others substitute somewhat healthier ingredients in places to make more calorie-friendly dressings. Rather than mayonnaise, the Caesar and Waldorf dressings have a yogurt base. The result is lighter, more delicate and, to my mind, totally preferable. There are many variations of the traditional Niçoise salad: I have opted to omit the red onions and potatoes, much preferring the salad without them, but by all means chuck 'em in if you wish, though remember that potatoes will add calories. Tabouleh and Baba Ghanoush take shape wrapped up in a fluffy flatbread — low calorie does not always mean low carb. Potatoes are part of my Irish heritage and I feel proud that we use this wonderful vegetable in such abundance. The humble spud has a very special place in my heart, not least because it is such a versatile vegetable. The potato salad, or Superb Spud Salad as I have lovingly named it, is a true delight.

These classics may be low calorie, but they are high impact — just as they should be!

purple kale and baby gem caesar salad

When you look at the components of a classic Caesar salad,
they don't appear to be all that exciting. The secret to a great Caesar,
however, is a great dressing, and here you will find just that. The inclusion
of purple kale is my own little flourish and is a delicious addition.
If you can't find any, green kale will suffice and, in the absence of either,
delicious baby gem will more than hold its own.

Serves 4 calories 285

Carbs 17g   Sugar 3.5g   Protein 14g   Fibre 4g   Fat 17g   Sat Fat 4.5g   Salt 2.9g

125g day-old sourdough bread
2 tablespoons olive oil
200g purple kale
200g baby gem lettuce leaves
50g anchovies
40g Parmesan

For the dressing (makes
    120ml)
3 anchovies (about 8–10g)
1 small garlic clove
3 thyme sprigs, leaves picked
    (optional)
10g Parmesan, finely grated
1½ tablespoons olive oil
3 tablespoons natural yogurt
1 teaspoon Worcestershire sauce
1 teaspoon Dijon mustard
juice of ½ lemon
salt and freshly ground black
    pepper

Preheat the oven to 200°C/gas mark 6.

Roughly tear the bread into sizeable chunks and place
on a baking tray. Coat with 1 tablespoon of olive oil
and bake in the oven for about 10 minutes until crispy.
Check regularly to ensure it doesn't burn.

Meanwhile, wash the kale under warm water to soften
the leaves. Dry thoroughly, coat with the remaining
tablespoon of olive oil and roast on another tray for
5–7 minutes. Remove from the oven and leave to cool.

To make the dressing, using a pestle and mortar,
pound the anchovies, garlic, thyme and a pinch of salt
until you have a paste. Add the remaining ingredients
and mix together. Season to taste. Remember,
anchovies are quite salty, so err on the side of caution
when seasoning.

Dress the kale and baby gem and top with the croutons
and anchovies. Use a cheese slice or potato peeler to
thinly shave the Parmesan and scatter all over the salad.

Tip: If you don't have a pestle and mortar, use a hand-
held blender.

greek salad

Red onions are usually found in a Greek salad but I am not a huge fan of them served raw because of their overpowering flavour and powerful aftertaste. Here, they appear in the dressing, in a supporting role rather than a main feature of the dish. They make the dressing more robust, but their flavour is mellowed and sweetened by the vinegar.

Serves 4

Carbs 7g   Sugar 7g   Protein 7g   Fibre 3g   Fat 14g   Sat Fat 5g   Salt 1g

650g tomatoes (I use mixed varieties)
1 medium cucumber, cut into sizeable chunks
1 baby gem lettuce, roughly chopped
10 Kalamata olives, pitted
2 oregano sprigs, leaves picked (optional)
125g feta cheese
pinch of dried oregano

For the dressing
¼ red onion, very finely chopped
2 tablespoons red wine vinegar
2 tablespoons olive oil
2 tablespoons water
salt and freshly ground black pepper

Begin by making the dressing. Mix all the ingredients together, season with a pinch of salt and pepper and set aside.

Prepare all the vegetables. Slice, quarter or halve the tomatoes, depending on size, and put in a large bowl with the cucumber, baby gem, olives and oregano leaves.

When ready to serve, dress the salad, crumble the feta cheese on top and sprinkle with the dried oregano.

niçoise salad

This recipe evokes memories of travelling around the South of France with some of my closest friends, especially Claire, who ate Nicoise for breakfast, lunch and dinner. Every time we ate this salad it would be beachside, sipping a glass of chilled rosé and feeling like life simply couldn't get any better!

Serves 4 calories 255 DF GF

Carbs 4g   Sugar 3.5g   Protein 22g   Fibre 3.5g   Fat 16g   Sat Fat 3g   Salt 2.9g

200g green beans (and yellow if you can find them)
2 medium free-range eggs
2 baby gem lettuce, roughly torn
250g mixed baby tomatoes, halved
16 Kalamata olives, pitted
200g best-quality tinned tuna, in brine
50g anchovies

For the dressing
3 tablespoons olive oil
2 tablespoons cold water
2 tablespoons white wine vinegar
1 tablespoon Dijon mustard
½ garlic clove, finely grated or chopped
3 tablespoons finely chopped herbs, such as flat-leaf parsley, basil and chives
salt and freshly ground black pepper

Bring a medium pot of water to a rolling boil and fill a bowl with ice-cold water. Blanch the beans for 3 minutes, remove with a slotted spoon and place in the bowl of cold water to refresh.

Bring the same water back to the boil and add the eggs. Cook for 6 minutes exactly. Meanwhile, drain the beans and pat dry with kitchen paper. Refill the bowl with cold water and when the eggs are ready, remove from the saucepan and place in the water to stop the cooking process. Gently crack the shells of the eggs with the back of a spoon and peel off the shell. Rinse under a little cold water to ensure all the shell is removed. Cut each one into quarters.

Mix all the dressing ingredients together and season to taste. Dress the beans, lettuce, tomatoes and olives, serve on individual plates or one large platter, and place the eggs, tuna and anchovies on top.

waldorf salad

This recipe is my adaptation of the original. The fresh dill brings the sweeter flavours of the apples and grapes back down to earth, adding what I feel is a necessary savoury note to the dish. The dressing is tangy and sour, with a little hit of maple syrup making a surprise but very welcome appearance!

Serves 4

calories 194   GF   V

Carbs 14g   Sugar 12.5g   Protein 4.5g   Fibre 3g   Fat 13g   Sat Fat 2g   Salt 0.3g

1 small pink lady apple
squeeze of lemon juice
1 small head of radicchio, leaves
   shredded
6 celery sticks, sliced
150g mixed seedless grapes
   (red, black, green), halved
60g walnuts, toasted
30g dill, fronds picked

For the dressing
2 tablespoons natural yogurt
2 tablespoons soured cream
2 tablespoons cider vinegar
1½ tablespoons English
   mustard
½ tablespoon maple syrup
   (alternatively use honey or
   agave nectar)
½ teaspoon freshly ground
   black pepper
generous pinch of salt

Halve, core and slice the apple and dress with the lemon juice. Put into a large bowl and add the radicchio, celery, grapes, walnuts and dill.

Mix the dressing ingredients together and taste for seasoning. Pour the dressing over the salad and mix thoroughly. Taste again to ensure there's enough seasoning in the dressing to complement the salad and add a little more salt and pepper if you feel it is needed.

panzanella

Panzanella is one of those recipes that tastes more beautiful than it sounds. How amazing can tomatoes, bread and basil really be? In truth, you won't believe how good it is until you try it. Use the best-quality ripe tomatoes you can find and the freshest basil, as well as some great sourdough. Good-quality extra virgin olive oil is integral to this recipe. You don't have to char the bread as it's not strictly traditional, but I like it. If your bread is too fresh, dry it out in a low oven (130°C/gas mark 1) for about 7 minutes.

Serves 4 calories 196 V VE

Carbs 20g   Sugar 6g   Protein 4g   Fibre 3g   Fat 10.5g   Sat Fat 1.5g   Salt 0.3g

125g stale sourdough bread, sliced
3½ tablespoons extra virgin olive oil
1½ tablespoons red wine vinegar
750g ripe tomatoes, sliced
20g basil, leaves picked
salt and freshly ground black pepper

Place a griddle pan over a high heat and, when smoking hot, grill the bread until nicely charred. When cool, tear into chunks and tip into a large bowl.

Five minutes before serving, dress the bread with the olive oil and red wine vinegar. Then add the tomatoes and toss. Leave for another few minutes to allow the bread to soften a little and soak up some flavour.

Finally, add the basil and season with a generous pinch of salt and pepper.

a very beautiful coleslaw

This is no ordinary coleslaw: it's stunning in appearance and even more so in flavour. Tofu makes it vegan and dairy free, and by no means compromises on the taste. I think the heat from the chilli makes the flavours of each vegetable sing, but do leave it out if you wish. I could eat this stuff by the bowlful and think that, with the variety of vegetables and textures, it makes a great salad dish in itself, but you can also serve it as a healthy side salad.

Serves 4 calories 143 GF V (VE and DF if using tofu)

Carbs 13g   Sugar 12.5g   Protein 6.5g   Fibre 8.5g   Fat 5.5g   Sat Fat 1.5g   Salt 0.6g

2 medium carrots, peeled
¼ small white cabbage (about 250g)
¼ small red cabbage (about 250g)
100g kale
1 small fennel bulb (about 200g)
10g flat-leaf parsley, leaves picked and roughly chopped
7 or 8 thyme sprigs, leaves picked and finely chopped

For the dressing
150g natural yogurt or silken tofu
juice of ½ lemon
1½ tablespoons cider vinegar
1½ tablespoons Dijon mustard
1 tablespoon olive oil
1 heaped teaspoon English mustard
¼–½ teaspoon chilli flakes
salt and freshly ground black pepper

Place the grater attachment on a food-processor and grate the carrot. Remove and add the thinnest slicer attachment and slice the white and red cabbage, kale and fennel. Tip out into a large bowl and add the herbs.

Mix all the dressing ingredients together, season to taste, pour over the vegetables and toss until thoroughly coated. Taste for seasoning and serve.

delicious egg salad with cress

My Mum has a unique talent for making mundane dishes sophisticated and special, and I have her to thank for this one. She does egg salad better than anyone I know: full of chunky pieces of egg, juicy tomatoes, crisp spring onion, fragrant parsley and crunchy lettuce, all brought together with the perfect amount of mayonnaise – enough to dress, not enough to drown.

Serves 4

Carbs 33g Sugar 5g Protein 13.5g Fibre 4g Fat 10.5g Sat Fat 3g Salt 2.4g

3 medium free-range eggs
15 cherry tomatoes, quartered
2 spring onions, finely chopped
small bunch of curly-leaf parsley, finely chopped
80g rocket, roughly chopped
salt and freshly ground black pepper

For the dressing
1 tablespoon mayonnaise
1 tablespoon crème fraîche
¾ tablespoon Dijon mustard
1½ teaspoons sherry vinegar
dash of Tabasco sauce (optional)

To serve
2 Dijon Brown Soda bread Scones (see page 88)
40g salad cress
40g Sweet Pickled Red Onions (see page 144, optional)

Bring a medium pan of water to the boil and add the eggs. Cook for exactly 8 minutes, then run under cold water to stop the eggs from cooking further.

Meanwhile, make the dressing. Mix together the mayonnaise, crème fraîche, Dijon mustard, sherry vinegar and Tabasco sauce, if using. Season to taste.

Using the back of a spoon, crack the shells of each egg all over and gently peel off. Rinse under cold water to remove any little bits of shell left behind. Cut each one in half lengthways and then each half into three. Put in a medium bowl and add the tomatoes, spring onions, parsley and rocket. Dress and season to taste.

To serve, cut each scone in half. Pile a nice spoonful of egg salad onto each one and garnish generously with salad cress, and sweet pickled red onions, if using.

Tip: Salad cress can be bought in most supermarkets growing in little pots. If you are sprouting your own mung beans (see page 12), they would be a delicious addition here.

dijon brown soda bread scones

Any variation of soda bread is a total cinch to whip up. With a kick of mustard, these scones are wonderfully savoury and will make a delicious addition to many of the salads in this book, particularly the Delicious Egg Salad with Cress (see page 86). In this recipe, they are shaped into larger rectangles, which are then halved and served with the egg salad. You can also cut the dough into four, which will give you smaller square scones. Simply cook them for 10–15 minutes instead.

Makes 2/Serves 4   calories 159 (V)

Carbs 30g   Sugar 1.8g   Protein 5.5g   Fibre 2.8g   Fat 1g   Sat Fat 0.3g   Salt 2g

80g wholemeal flour
80g white flour
3 thyme sprigs, leaves picked
1 teaspoon salt
½ teaspoon bicarbonate of
  soda
¾ tablespoon Dijon mustard
½ teaspoon English mustard
100ml buttermilk, plus extra
  for brushing

Preheat the oven to 190°C/gas mark 5. Line a baking tray with parchment paper.

Mix the flours, thyme, salt, bicarbonate of soda and mustards together in a medium bowl. Pour in the buttermilk and mix gently until you have a soft, slightly sticky dough.

Turn out onto a lightly floured surface and shape into a rectangle about 2cm deep. Slice in half and place onto the baking tray. Brush with a little buttermilk, or egg wash if you have it, sprinkle with a little salt and bake for 15–20 minutes, until golden brown on top. Transfer to a wire rack to cool.

superb spud salad with flaked salmon and pickled cucumber

Potato salad doesn't get better than this! If, like my Mum, you have a habit of cooking too many potatoes, this is a great recipe for leftovers. Another nice twist, if you're serving this with barbecued food, is to finish the potatoes above the hot coals, charring them a little to give them a delicious smoky flavour.

Serves 4 GF

Carbs 25g   Sugar 6g   Protein 14g   Fibre 4g   Fat 9g   Sat Fat 2.5g   Salt 0.5g

500g baby new potatoes
1 red onion
2 tablespoons red wine vinegar
2 medium free-range eggs or
   6 quail eggs
70g watercress
25g flat-leaf parsley, roughly
   chopped
100g cooked flaked salmon
   (you can buy cooked salmon
   in most big supermarkets)
100g Pickled Chargrilled
   Cucumbers (see page 153)
salt and freshly ground black
   pepper

For the dressing
1 heaped teaspoon capers,
   roughly chopped
3 cornichons, roughly chopped
5 or 6 dill sprigs, finely
   chopped
zest and juice of ½ lemon
1 tablespoon crème fraîche
1 tablespoon Dijon mustard
1 teaspoon English mustard

Put the potatoes in a large saucepan, cover with water, add a generous pinch of salt, bring to the boil and simmer for 20–30 minutes or until soft. When ready, drain and set aside to cool.

Slice the red onion very thinly and soak in the red wine vinegar for 10 minutes.

Simmer the eggs in the same water as the potatoes (you can do this while the potatoes are cooking). For quail eggs, cook for exactly 3 minutes, and for hen eggs, 8 minutes. When ready, immerse in ice-cold water to stop them from cooking any further. When cool enough to handle, remove the shells, and cut each egg into six (or two if using quail eggs).

To make the dressing, simply mix all the ingredients together and season to taste. To assemble the salad, mix the potatoes, onion, watercress and parsley in a bowl. Pour over the dressing and toss. Serve with the eggs, salmon and pickled cucumbers.

Tip: If you have made the sweet pickled red onions (see page 149), you can use these here instead of fresh sliced red onion.

tabouleh flatbreads with baba ghanoush

When I eat in a Lebanese restaurant, these two classic dishes are my favourite combination. Although some time and effort goes into creating baba ghanoush, it's worth every second: it has one of the most addictive and truly delicious flavours I can think of.

Serves 4

Carbs 34g   Sugar 7g   Protein 10.5g   Fibre 9.5g   Fat 11g   Sat Fat 1.5g   Salt 0.4g

30g bulgar wheat

100g flat-leaf parsley, finely chopped

40g mint, leaves picked and finely chopped

350g cucumber, halved, deseeded and diced

100g cherry or baby plum tomatoes, halved

juice of 1 lemon

1 tablespoon olive oil

2 Lebanese flatbreads, or pitta breads, halved (about 70g each), to serve

¼ jar Sweet Pickled Red Onions (see page 149), or 3 spring onions, finely chopped, to garnish

salt and freshly ground black pepper

For the baba ghanoush

2 medium aubergines

1 head of garlic

1½ tablespoons tahini

1 tablespoon olive oil

First make the baba ghanoush; the flavour is best when this is done the night before you want to serve it. Char the aubergines over the naked flame of a gas hob for about 30 minutes, until the skins are crisp, brittle and totally blackened, and the centre so soft the aubergines are collapsing in on themselves. Transfer to a bowl, cover in clingfilm and allow to cool completely.

Preheat the oven to 200°C/gas mark 6.

Wrap the garlic in foil, place on a baking tray and roast for 40 minutes.

Gently peel the skin from the aubergines and place in a bowl. Squeeze the soft flesh from the garlic cloves and mash it into the aubergine. Add the tahini and olive oil and beat everything together until you have a nice smooth purée. Season to taste.

Boil the bulgar wheat in salted water for 15 minutes. Refresh under cold water to stop the cooking process and set aside to drain thoroughly. Transfer the bulgar to a large bowl and stir in the parsley, mint, cucumber and tomatoes. Dress with the lemon juice, olive oil and a good pinch of salt and pepper.

Heat the flatbreads in a moderate oven and serve stuffed with the tabouleh and baba ghanoush and garnished with sweet pickled red onion.

celeriac remoulade with salt cod croquettes

There are few things as simple and perfect as a celeriac remoulade.
This version uses yogurt in place of mayonnaise in the dressing, and is
even better served alongside these Nordic-style croquettes.

Serves 4 calories 299

Carbs 21g   Sugar 4g   Protein 44g   Fibre 6g   Fat 3g   Sat Fat 0.7g   Salt 3.5g

For the croquettes

250g salt cod

250g potatoes, cut into small
    cubes

5g chives, finely chopped

zest of ½ lemon

2 tablespoons panko
    breadcrumbs

olive oil

salt and freshly ground black
    pepper

For the dressing

2 tablespoons natural yogurt

1 tablespoon Dijon mustard

juice of ½ lemon

For the remoulade

350g celeriac, sliced into
    matchsticks (either by hand
    or in a food-processor)

28g flat-leaf parsley, finely
    chopped

juice of 1 lemon

2 tablespoons natural yogurt

1 tablespoon Dijon mustard

1 teaspoon English mustard

Soak the cod for 24 hours in cold water, refreshing the
water a few times. Drain and pat dry with kitchen paper.

Preheat the oven to 200°C/gas mark 6. Transfer
the fish to a baking tray and bake for 8–10 minutes.
Remove from the oven and allow to cool.

Boil the potatoes in salted water for about 10 minutes,
or until nice and soft. Drain and return them to the pan
to dry off in their own steam for about 5 minutes. Mash
until smooth, flake in the cod and add the chopped
chives and lemon zest. Mix together and season to taste.

Divide the mixture into eight and shape into little rolls.
Coat with the panko breadcrumbs and refrigerate for at
least 30 minutes before cooking.

Mix together the dressing ingredients, and add a pinch
of salt and pepper. Set aside. Gently mix together the
remoulade ingredients with your hands, making sure
the celeriac is evenly coated.

Drizzle a little olive oil into a large frying pan over a
high heat. Add the croquettes and fry for about 6–8
minutes, turning constantly to ensure they brown and
become crisp on all sides. Serve with the remoulade,
with a little dressing drizzled on top or served
alongside. They are also delicious served with sriracha.

show-off salads

Salads are great for entertaining. They are generally easy to put together and can create a glorious display on any table. The recipes in this chapter are fit for a feast, designed to take centre stage. Imagine them on beautiful plates impressively cascading down buffet tables, bursting with swagger and personality. They also help you maintain a calorie controlled diet even when entertaining — an occasion that threatens to throw you off course.

But although they are particularly stunning in appearance, they are no more challenging to create than any other recipe in this book. Fennel, nectarine and watercress are speckled with beautiful black quinoa and the whole dish is finished with a touch of truffle honey for a bit of shameless indulgence. Beetroot gets a spicy makeover, balanced with crunchy pak choi and succulent, soft-centred ramen eggs (which couldn't be easier to make!) — a feast for the eyes as well as the taste buds. Tiger prawns are teamed with a bejewelled roasted red pepper, herb and pearl barley salad. Chicken skewers marinated with honey, soy, ginger, and five-spice are enveloped in crunchy cos lettuce leaves to create the most elegant of salad wraps.

These dishes are nothing short of simple sophistication.

spicy beetroot and pak choi with ramen eggs and sriracha

This salad is for those of you who like your spice hot! The roasted beetroot is fabulously fiery and counterbalanced perfectly by soft-centred ramen eggs (a doddle to make!) and crunchy pak choi.

Serves 4 calories 207 DF V

Carbs 19g   Sugar 14g   Protein 10.5g   Fibre 2.5g   Fat 9.5g   Sat Fat 2.2g   Salt 3.6g

2½ tablespoons light soy sauce
  or tamari
1 tablespoon gochujang
  (Korean chilli paste)
1 teaspoon chilli oil (optional)
4 medium beetroot
1 tablespoon olive oil
3 heads of pak choi, sliced
  lengthways
½ tablespoon black or white
  sesame seeds
2 tablespoons sriracha

For the ramen eggs
90ml sake
45ml light soy sauce or tamari
45ml mirin
4 medium free-range eggs

Tip: Raw beetroot takes quite a while to roast in the oven. If strapped for time, buy ready-cooked vacuum-packed beetroot and roast with the marinade for 10 minutes.

The ramen eggs are best if marinated for 24 hours. Mix the sake, soy sauce or tamari and mirin together in a bowl deep enough to submerge the eggs in.

Bring a large saucepan of water to the boil and cook the eggs for 6 minutes exactly, then plunge them into a bowl of ice-cold water for a minute or so. While the eggs are still warm but cool enough to handle, lightly crack the shells with the back of a spoon, peel them under water then add to the marinade. Put a plate or something similar over the bowl to ensure the eggs remain fully immersed. Leave to marinate for at least 3 hours or overnight, if possible.

Preheat the oven to 200°C/gas mark 6. In a small bowl, mix together the soy sauce, gochujang and chilli oil, if using.

Peel the beetroot and cut each into eight wedges. Toss with the olive oil and place on a large baking tray. Cover with foil and roast for 50 minutes. Remove from the oven, coat with the soy and gochujang mixture, and then cook for a further 10 minutes, keeping an eye on it to make sure that the sauce doesn't catch and burn.

Remove the eggs from the marinade and cut in half. Serve the beetroot warm or cold with the pak choi, egg, a generous sprinkle of sesame seeds and the sriracha sauce.

green goodness

When I think about energising and invigorating food, this kind of dish springs to mind. It's utterly wholesome, full of goodness and gives tired bodies a welcome hit of energy. I adore the combination of avocado and grapefruit, and here you have it within the dressing as well as the salad.

Serves 4   (VE if using agave nectar)

Carbs 21g Sugar 6.5g Protein 10g Fibre 7.5g Fat 6.5g Sat Fat 1.5g Salt trace

400g can black beans, drained and rinsed under cold water
100g frozen peas
50g edamame beans
35g coriander, roughly chopped
zest of 1 lime
1 courgette (about 150g)
½ pink grapefruit
2 baby gem lettuce
½ small avocado, stoned, peeled, sliced and dressed with a little lime juice

For the dressing
½ small avocado, peeled
juice of ½ pink grapefruit
juice of 1 lime
1 teaspoon agave nectar or honey
½ red chilli, deseeded
salt and freshly ground black pepper

Put all the dressing ingredients in a small food-processor or blender and blitz until smooth. Season to taste.

Put the black beans, peas, edamame beans, coriander and lime zest in a large bowl. Grate the courgette using a food-processor or by hand. Segment the grapefruit using a very sharp knife and add to the bowl along with the grated courgette. Toss with half of the dressing.

Serve with the baby gem and avocado and the remaining dressing drizzled all over.

sticky five-spice chicken wraps

I know there is a long list of ingredients here, but don't be intimidated:
this recipe looks scarier than it is, and these chicken skewers are to die for!

Serves 4 calories 193

Carbs 7g   Sugar 5.5g   Protein 20g   Fibre 1g   Fat 9g   Sat Fat 1.5g   Salt 4.1g

4 boneless, skinless chicken
   thighs
1 lemongrass stalk
3 garlic cloves
25g fresh ginger, chopped
2 tablespoons fish sauce
½ teaspoon honey
1½ teaspoons five-spice powder
1 tablespoon oyster sauce
   (optional)
1–2 tablespoons sunflower oil
150g beansprouts
7–8 Thai basil sprigs
20g coriander, leaves picked
20g mint, leaves picked
4 large romaine or cos leaves

For the nuoc cham dressing
1 garlic clove
25g fresh ginger, finely grated
1 red chilli, deseeded and
   roughly chopped
¾ tablespoon caster sugar
juice of 1½ limes
2 tablespoons fish sauce

For the peanut sauce
½ tablespoon peanut butter
½ tablespoon soy sauce
1 teaspoon fish sauce
juice of ½ lime

Bash the chicken thighs between two large pieces of
parchment paper until really thin. Slice each one into
three strips about 1–2 cm wide and set aside. Soak four
wooden skewers in cold water for at least 20 minutes.

Pound the lemongrass, garlic and ginger using a pestle
and mortar until you have a rough paste, or chop by
hand as finely as possible. Add the fish sauce, honey,
five-spice powder and oyster sauce (if using) and
mix well. Pour over the chicken and marinate for a
minimum of 2 hours, or ideally overnight.

For the nuoc cham dressing, pound the garlic, ginger,
chilli and sugar in a pestle and mortar until you have a
smooth paste. Add the lime juice and fish sauce and mix.
Combine all the peanut sauce ingredients together with
½ tablespoon warm water and mix until smooth.

Thread the chicken onto the skewers and allow to come
to room temperature for 10 minutes or so. Place a
medium frying or griddle pan over a high heat and add
the sunflower oil. When really hot, add the chicken
and cook for 10 minutes, turning regularly so that it
becomes nicely charred and crispy all over.

Dress the beansprouts and herbs with half the dressing,
reserving the other half for dipping. Place a generous
spoonful of the beansprout mix into a lettuce leaf, top
with chicken, drizzle with the peanut sauce and serve
with the remaining dressing.

turmeric and ginger chicken salad

This salad is as vibrant as they come, in appearance and flavour.
If you are ever planning a detox, this is the salad for the job.

Serves 4

Carbs 14g   Sugar 6g   Protein 23g   Fibre 4g   Fat 4g   Sat Fat 0.5g   Salt 0.2g

1 large or 2 small chicken
   breasts (about 250g)
60g black quinoa
150g baby spinach, finely
   shredded
1 red pepper, deseeded and
   thinly sliced
100g green beans, finely
   chopped
50g alfalfa sprouts, or whatever
   sprouts you have grown or
   can find
5g chives, finely chopped
10g flat-leaf parsley, finely
   chopped
1 lime, cut into wedges, to serve

For the dressing
100g tofu
25g fresh turmeric root (or
   1 heaped teaspoon of ground
   turmeric)
15g fresh ginger, peeled
1 tablespoon maple syrup
juice of 1 lime
salt and freshly ground black
   pepper

Bring a large pot of salted water to the boil. Add the
chicken breasts and quinoa. Simmer the chicken for
10 minutes then remove and set aside to cool. Allow
the quinoa to cook for a further 10 minutes then drain
into a sieve and run under cold water to cool and stop
it from cooking any further.

Meanwhile, make the dressing. In a small food-
processor, blitz everything together until smooth.
Taste for seasoning: if it is too sour, add a touch more
maple syrup; if it is too sweet, add an extra squeeze of
lime juice.

When the chicken is cool, finely chop and put into
a bowl. Toss with a few spoonfuls of the dressing.
Arrange everything on a large platter, and serve the
dressing alongside to be poured all over. Add a squeeze
of lime for the perfect finishing touch.

wilted chard and beef

I can never resist a bunch of rainbow chard — its psychedelic yellow, pink and red stalks are things of absolute beauty and utterly mesmerising. If you can't find them, use pak choi instead.

Serves 4 calories 222 DF (GF if using tamari)

Carbs 10g Sugar 4g Protein 24g Fibre 0.5g Fat 9.5g Sat Fat 3g Salt 3.7g

1 teaspoon sesame oil
800g rainbow chard, stalks cut into 2.5cm pieces and leaves finely shredded
5 tablespoons light soy sauce or tamari
1 teaspoon rice wine vinegar
1 teaspoon olive oil
2 fillet steaks (approx. 350g)
1 teaspoon chilli flakes
40g mint, leaves picked
30g Thai basil, leaves picked
zest of ½ lemon
1 red chilli, finely sliced
1 tablespoon black sesame seeds
salt and freshly ground black pepper

Heat the sesame oil and 1 tablespoon of water in a large frying pan. Add the chard, stir a little to distribute the heat and place a lid on top. Allow to steam for a few minutes, then stir again, and continue to do so until the chard has wilted and the stalks are softened, about 5 minutes. Add the soy sauce and rice wine vinegar and cook for a further 2–3 minutes.

Rub the olive oil all over the steaks then season with the chilli flakes and some pepper. Heat a griddle pan over a high heat and, when smoking hot, cook the steaks for about 3 minutes on each side. Rest for 5 minutes before slicing thinly.

To serve, place the warm chard on a plate and top with the fresh herbs and sliced steak. Finish with a scattering of lemon zest, fresh chilli and sesame seeds.

roasted red pepper and pearl barley with barbecued prawns

Try to get your hands on big juicy fresh tiger prawns from your fishmonger. They are not the cheapest, but they are worth every penny. If you are not a fan of fish, use the marinade on some chicken thighs and you will have a dish just as fab!

Serves 4

Carbs 16g   Sugar 6g   Protein 38g   Fibre 3.5g   Fat 2.5g   Sat Fat 0.5g   Salt 1.8g

8 raw tiger prawns, unpeeled
50g pearl barley
I vegetable stock cube
8 wedges of Roasted Pickled
    Red Peppers (see page 154)
    or 2 fresh red peppers
50g flat-leaf parsley, leaves
    picked
2 tarragon sprigs, leaves picked
10g dill, fronds picked
50g rocket
I quantity Roasted Red Pepper,
    Basil and Chilli Dressing
    (see page 145)
lemon wedges, to serve

For the marinade
I lime, halved
2 garlic cloves, chopped
I tablespoon smoked paprika
½ teaspoon chilli flakes
    (optional)
I teaspoon freshly ground black
    pepper
I tablespoon olive oil

To marinate the prawns, juice one half of the lime and finely chop the other, pith and all. In a large bowl, mix together the marinade ingredients with 2 tablespoons of water. Stir to make a paste. Toss the prawns in the marinade, ensuring they are thoroughly coated. Refrigerate while you prepare the rest of the dish.

Put the pearl barley in a pan, cover with water, add the stock cube and cook according to the packet instructions. Drain in a sieve and run under cold water to cool and stop the barley from cooking further.

If using fresh red peppers, preheat the oven to 200°C and roast the peppers for 30 minutes until blackened. Transfer to a bowl, cover with clingfilm and set aside until cool enough to handle, then peel off the skin and tear the pepper into long strips, discarding the seeds. Put the pepper in a bowl with the cooked barley, herbs and rocket.

Cook the prawns on a barbecue, or in a griddle pan over a very high heat, for 7–8 minutes.

Dress the salad and serve immediately with the barbecued prawns and wedges of lemon.

gravlax, pickled chargrilled cucumber and grapefruit soured cream

There is nothing complicated about making gravlax — it simply requires time. You don't even have to do anything within that time — just wait, patiently, for a little bit of magic to happen.

Serves 4 calories 183 GF

Carbs 4g Sugar 4g Protein 14g Fibre 1g Fat 12g Sat Fat 3g Salt 2.5g

For the gravlax
zest of ½ grapefruit
1½ tablespoons charcoal salt
1½ tablespoons soft brown
  sugar
250–300g tail end piece
  of salmon (ask your
  fishmonger)
2 tablespoons fresh grapefruit
  juice
20g dill, fronds finely chopped

For the grapefruit soured cream
50g soured cream
zest of ¼ grapefruit
1 teaspoon fresh grapefruit
  juice
¼ teaspoon sherry vinegar
salt and freshly ground black
  pepper

For the salad
½ jar Pickled Chargrilled
  Cucumber (about 200g,
  see page 153)
2 small punnets of cress
sea salt and freshly ground
  black pepper

Mix together the grapefruit zest, salt and sugar. Place the salmon on a large piece of parchment paper and cover with the salt and sugar mixture, followed by the grapefruit juice and finally the dill.

Fold the parchment all around the salmon so that it is totally encased. Wrap tightly in foil and place on a plate. Put another plate on top and weigh it down with something heavy. Refrigerate for 36 hours, then rinse under cold water and pat dry.

Mix the soured cream, grapefruit zest and juice and sherry vinegar together and season lightly. Taste the seasoning and adjust to your liking if necessary. Mix the pickled cucumber with the cress.

To serve, slice the gravlax as thinly as possible and serve alongside the salad and grapefruit soured cream and a sprinkle of salt and pepper.

Tip: Look for charcoal salt in supermarkets, delis and online. If you can't find it, you can use plain sea salt instead.

asparagus and smoked pickled tomatoes with boquerones and basil

I love a dish that gets a reaction from people, and when I served this salad for the first time, there was a lot of 'Wow, what is that?' whenever someone unexpectedly bit into a smoked pickled tomato. To look at it is simple, to taste it is something entirely different. Boquerones are Spanish anchovies, white in colour, larger in size and less salty than the more common variety you buy in tins or jars.

Serves 4 calories 109 DF GF

Carbs 5.5g   Sugar 5.5g   Protein 6g   Fibre 2.5g   Fat 6.5g   Sat Fat 1g   Salt 2g

200g Pickled Smoked Cherry
  Tomatoes (see page 153),
  halved
350g yellow cherry tomatoes,
  halved
150g asparagus, shaved with a
  potato peeler
12 boquerones (about 55g)
small bunch of basil, leaves
  picked and roughly torn
1½ tablespoons extra virgin
  olive oil
juice of ½ lemon
salt and freshly ground black
  pepper

Arrange the cherry tomatoes, asparagus, boquerones and basil leaves on a large platter and dress with the olive oil and lemon juice. Finish with a touch of salt and pepper.

blackened green beans and sesame-seared tuna with tomato vinaigrette

This salad uses the Pickled Smoked Cherry Tomatoes on page 155, but you can still make it without: simply use fresh cherry tomatoes, roasting a quarter of them for 5 minutes in a really hot oven to soften them before passing them though a sieve and follow the recipe below, using sherry vinegar instead of the pickling liquor.

Serves 4

Carbs 7g Sugar 5g Protein 27g Fibre 7g Fat 14g Sat Fat 2g Salt 0.2g

150g Pickled Smoked Cherry Tomatoes (see page 155)
2 tablespoons olive oil, plus extra for frying
½ tablespoon pickling liquor (or sherry vinegar)
400g green beans, trimmed
300g runner beans, halved lengthways
2 tablespoons sesame seeds
350g fresh tuna steak
salt and freshly ground black pepper

First make the vinaigrette. Place a quarter of the tomatoes in a sieve over a bowl and mash with the back of a spoon, pressing out all the juices. You should have about 1½ tablespoons of juice. Add 1 tablespoon of olive oil and ½ tablespoon of pickling liquor and mix until emulsified. Lightly season with a pinch of salt and pepper.

Dress the beans with the remaining tablespoon of olive oil and a generous pinch of salt and pepper. Place a griddle pan over a high heat and, when smoking hot, add half the green and runner beans and cook until lightly charred. Remove, and cook the second batch.

Spread out the sesame seeds on a flat surface, such as a chopping board or baking tray, and season with a pinch of salt and pepper. Press both sides of the tuna into the seeds to ensure it is evenly and thoroughly coated.

Heat a splash of oil in the pan and, when smoking hot, cook the tuna for no more than 20 seconds on each side. Allow to rest for a couple of minutes before slicing.

Pour the tomato vinaigrette over the beans and remaining tomatoes and toss to combine. Serve alongside the seared tuna.

brussels sprouts, feta, wild rice, chestnuts and pomegranate

Brussels sprouts: the ultimate acquired taste. I love them blanched and fried in loads of butter and fatty crispy bacon – one of my favourite Christmas treats. But they are beautiful in their humble and somewhat misunderstood raw state, too. They are the unapologetic star of this salad – and served like this, you'll struggle to comprehend why they are so loathed by so many.

Serves 4

Carbs 28g   Sugar 11g   Protein 10.5g   Fibre 8g   Fat 12g   Sat Fat 4.5g   Salt 0.8g

50g wild rice

4 rosemary sprigs

½ tablespoon olive oil

300g Brussels sprouts

100g cooked vacuum-packed
chestnuts, roughly chopped

28g flat-leaf parsley, roughly
chopped

seeds from ½ medium
pomegranate (about 100g)

100g feta cheese

salt and freshly ground black
pepper

For the dressing (makes
130ml)

1½ tablespoons tahini

1 tablespoon agave nectar

1 tablespoon wholegrain
mustard

3 oregano sprigs, leaved picked
and finely chopped

1 tablespoon freshly squeezed
orange juice

juice of ½ lemon

2 tablespoons hot water

Preheat the oven to 180°C/gas mark 4.

Cook the rice according to the packet instructions. When cooked, drain and rinse under cold water to cool. Set aside.

Dress the rosemary with the olive oil and season with salt and pepper. Place on a baking tray and roast for 10 minutes, checking it regularly to ensure it doesn't burn. When ready, set aside to cool.

To make the dressing, mix everything together and season to taste.

Slice the Brussels sprouts in a food-processor fitted with the slicer attachment, or thinly slice by hand. Put them in a large bowl with the rice, chestnuts, parsley and three-quarters of the pomegranate seeds. Pour over the dressing and gently toss the salad so that everything is generously coated.

Serve topped with crumbled feta cheese, the remaining pomegranate seeds and some crispy roasted rosemary.

fennel and nectarine with black quinoa, watercress and goat's cheese

Crunchy aniseedy fennel, soft sweet nectarine, peppery watercress and fragrant dill, topped with creamy goat's cheese; showing off doesn't look or taste better than this!

Serves 4 calories 226 GF V

Carbs 19g   Sugar 12g   Protein 10g   Fibre 5g   Fat 12g   Sat Fat 5g   Salt 0.4g

60g black quinoa

1 medium fennel bulb (about 250g), cut into quarters

2 large ripe nectarines, halved, stoned and sliced thinly

5 or 6 dill sprigs, fronds roughly chopped

50g watercress

1½ tablespoons extra virgin olive oil

juice of 1 lemon

100g soft goat's cheese

1 teaspoon truffle honey (optional)

salt and freshly ground black pepper

Place the quinoa in a saucepan and cover with 140ml of water, bring to the boil and simmer, covered, for 15 minutes. Allow to cool in the saucepan — it will continue cooking in the steam.

Use the thinnest slicer attachment on a food-processor, or a mandolin, to slice the fennel. Place in a medium bowl with the nectarines, cooled quinoa, dill and watercress.

Dress with olive oil and lemon juice and season generously with salt and pepper. Serve with the goat's cheese crumbled on top with a drizzle of truffle honey, if using.

Tip: Plain honey or hazelnut agave nectar, see page 148, can be used instead of truffle honey.

crudités salad

This is a celebration of vegetables in all of their raw beauty. The recipe is far from set in stone — use whatever vegetables you love most, or what is in season. Choose which dips or dressings that appeal to you most and have fun creating stunning displays of gorgeous ingredients.

Serves 6
(calories per portion for the veg)

Carbs 8.5g   Sugar 7.5g   Protein 3g   Fibre 3.5g   Fat 1g   Sat Fat 0g   Salt 0.2g

1 bunch of radishes, halved or quartered (about 350g)

200g heirloom carrots, quartered lengthways

4 Lebanese cucumbers, quartered lengthways (or use standard cucumbers)

1 head of red chicory, leaves picked

150g sugarsnap peas

3 beetroot, mixed colours, peeled and sliced

4 celery sticks, halved lengthways and cut into 3

Arrange all the vegetables on a big platter and serve with your dips of choice.

Choose two of the following dips:
Chermoula Dressing (see page 144) [DF, GF, V, VE]
Salsa Verde (see page 143) [DF, GF]
Roasted Red Pepper, Basil and Chilli Dressing (see page 145) [DF, GF, V, VE]
Sumac, Chilli and Lemon Yogurt Dressing (see page 145) [GF, V]
Blue Cheese Dressing (see page 148) [GF]

fruit salads

This chapter contains sweet fruit salads, as well as savoury salads adorned with fruit. A fruit salad is a very wonderful thing, and it's as good for breakfast as it is for dessert. It can be traditional and simple or something a little more unique and unusual. A hint of chilli and lime marries beautifully with the sweetness of mango and pineapple to make a light and refreshing dessert. Yuzu and pistachios adorn juicy melon for a delectable breakfast full of goodness. A summer berry salad finds its place in an ice-cream cone packed with blackberry sorbet — a deliciously healthy and fun way to cool down on warm days.

Fruit adds a layer of beauty to salads that few other ingredients can, and savoury salads embellished with fruits are among my favourites. Blood oranges and chicory are a match made in heaven and, adorned garnished with pecorino and hazelnuts, make a salad fit for kings. Soft succulent figs melt into peppery land cress with goat's cheese, while a touch a pink grapefruit teamed with coriander and fennel shares its plate with some home-smoked rainbow trout. And succulent crispy duck teamed with juicy pomelo is the kind of dish nobody wants to share.

Fruit makes simple salads sensational and ordinary salads outstanding.

roasted figs and goat's cheese with hazelnut and honeycomb

Land cress may be hard to come by, but it is perfectly substituted by watercress, or a mixture of watercress and rocket (sometimes I find watercress on its own too overpowering.) All these salad greens are fiery and peppery, which is just what's needed to balance the sweetness of the figs. I use honey still in its comb, breaking it into chunks so that it becomes an integral part of the salad. It's amazing and worth a try if you have never had it before.

Serves 4 calories 237 GF V

Carbs 20g   Sugar 20g   Protein 7g   Fibre 2g   Fat 14g   Sat Fat 4g   Salt 0.3g

125g baby figs, halved (alternatively use 3 regular figs, quartered)
2½ tablespoons balsamic vinegar
40g blanched hazelnuts
120g land cress (or a mix of watercress and rocket)
70g firm goat's cheese, sliced
30g honeycomb (or 2 tablespoons runny honey)
1 tablespoon extra virgin olive oil
celery salt (or regular sea salt)
freshly ground black pepper

Preheat the oven to 200°C/gas mark 6.

Place the figs on a roasting tray, drizzle with a tablespoon of balsamic vinegar and season with salt and pepper. Roast for 10 minutes.

Place the hazelnuts in a dry frying pan over a medium heat and toast until golden brown. Transfer to a chopping board and roughly chop when cool enough to handle.

Arrange the land cress on each plate, along with the roasted figs, chopped hazelnuts and goat's cheese. Break the honeycomb into small chunks all over the salad (this is a bit messy but I quite enjoy it!) and finish with a drizzle of the remaining balsamic vinegar and olive oil. Season with a generous pinch of celery salt and freshly ground black pepper.

fennel, pink grapefruit, coriander and chilli with smoked trout

This salad is light, crisp and refreshing, designed for a sunny day and a chilled glass of sauvignon blanc — and for moments when you are just feeling particularly fond of yourself. It shows you how to smoke fish in the comfort of your own kitchen, which is really fun to do, and definitely worth the effort.

Serves 4   calories 155   DF   GF

Carbs 7g Sugar 7g Protein 15g Fibre 4g Fat 6.5g Sat Fat 1g Salt 0.2g

2 rainbow trout fillets, skin on (about 250–300g)
4 baby fennel (about 300g)
2 pink grapefruit
1½ tablespoons Lemon and Lime Vinaigrette (see page 142)

For the smoker
large handful of dry rice
3 English breakfast tea bags (feel free to experiment with different flavours)

To garnish
5g coriander, finely chopped
pinch of chilli flakes

First prepare your 'smoker'. Line a frying pan or wok with three layers of foil and scatter the rice and tea bags on top. Place over a high heat. Don't worry if the rice pops and blackens a little — this is totally normal.

Place the fish, skin side down, on a wire rack big enough to rest on top of the wok or frying pan. When you see smoke starting to rise, place the rack on top and cover with a few layers of foil to trap in the smoke. Smoke for 8 minutes, then turn off the heat and allow the fish to cool on the rack while still covered. This step can be done up to a day in advance. Simply refrigerate the fish once cooled, and bring back to room temperature before using.

Finely slice the fennel and put it in a medium bowl. To segment the grapefruit, slice the skin from the fruit, removing as much pith as possible. Then cut out each segment; use the membrane as a guideline, slicing in between it with the sharpest knife you have.

Dress the fennel and grapefruit with the lemon and lime vinaigrette, garnish with coriander and chilli flakes, and serve with flakes of smoked trout.

melon, mint and pistachios

Chilling this salad will make it more refreshing on warm summer days, but it is not strictly necessary if you don't have the time.

Serves 4 calories 107   DF GF V VE

Carbs 12g Sugar 12g Protein 3g Fibre 1g Fat 5g Sat Fat 0.7g Salt 0g

1 melon, such as honeydew or
    piel de sapo (about 1–1.5kg),
    halved and seeded
2 tablespoons yuzu juice
zest and juice of 1 lime
1 teaspoon vanilla bean paste
30 mint leaves, finely shredded
40g shelled pistachios, roughly
    chopped, to garnish

Carve out the flesh of the melon using a melon baller. Otherwise, peel and roughly chop into 2cm cubes. Put the melon in a bowl with the yuzu, lime juice and vanilla bean paste. Mix well and refrigerate for about 2 hours. Just before serving, stir in the mint. Serve garnished with the pistachios and grated lime zest.

Tip: If you omit the pistachios, these ingredients can be blended together to make a delicious smoothie.

watermelon and courgette with feta and mint

This is my go-to salad on a hot summer's day. The flavours are a marriage made in heaven – refreshing yet punchy and wonderfully satisfying. Salty, creamy feta with juicy sweet watermelon; what's not to love?

Serves 4 calories 201   DF GF V VE

Carbs 13g Sugar 11g Protein 7g Fibre 2g Fat 13.5g Sat Fat 3.5g Salt 0.5g

900g watermelon (500g flesh)
1 yellow courgette (about 250g)
10 Kalamata olives, halved and
    pitted
30g pumpkin seeds
70g rocket
15g mint, leaves finely shredded
50g feta cheese
1½ tablespoons balsamic vinegar
2 tablespoons olive oil
1 teaspoon wholegrain mustard
salt and pepper

Remove the skin from the watermelon and cut into 2cm cubes. Use a potato peeler to peel long strips or ribbons of courgette. Add to a bowl along with the watermelon, olives, pumpkin seeds, rocket and mint. Crumble the feta cheese into the bowl.

Put the balsamic vinegar, olive oil and mustard in a jar and season. Screw on the lid and shake until totally emulsified. Pour all over the salad, toss until everything is thoroughly coated and season again. Serve immediately.

pineapple and mango with chilli, mint and lime

If you find the idea of using chilli alongside fruit alarming, reserve judgement: teamed with the sweetness of the sugar and fruit it creates the most amazing flavour sensation.

Serves 4

Carbs 30g   Sugar 25g   Protein 1g   Fibre 6g   Fat 0.5g   Sat Fat 0g   Salt 1.9g

1 medium pineapple
2 medium underripe mangoes
2 tablespoons caster sugar
½ red chilli, roughly chopped
1½ teaspoons salt
5g mint, leaves picked and
  finely shredded
5 fresh kaffir lime leaves, finely
  shredded (optional)
lime wedges

Peel and slice the pineapple and mango and put into a large bowl.

Using a pestle and mortar, grind the sugar, chilli and salt until you have a rough paste. Scatter over the fruit and toss to combine. Garnish with the mint and lime leaves (if using) and serve with lime wedges.

green papaya, mango and rare beef

Green papayas and mangoes can be found in Asian supermarkets, but if you don't have one locally, look out for underripe fruits instead.

Serves 4   calories 279 | DF | GF

Carbs 25g   Sugar 19g   Protein 16g   Fibre 7g   Fat 11g   Sat Fat 2.5g   Salt 1.2g

3 spring onions, trimmed,
   halved and julienned
½ tablespoon olive oil
180g skirt steak
1 green or underripe papaya
   (about 350g), peeled and
   deseeded
1 small green or underripe
   mango (about 450g), peeled
   and stone removed
30g mint, leaves picked
30g coriander, leaves picked
salt and freshly ground black
   pepper

For the dressing
1 small garlic clove
1 red bird's eye chilli
1 tablespoon caster sugar
juice of 2 limes
1 tablespoon fish sauce

To garnish
2 tablespoons mixed black and
   white sesame seeds
2 tablespoons crispy fried
   shallots (optional)
20g roasted peanuts, roughly
   chopped
1 red chilli, finely sliced

Place the julienned spring onions into a bowl of ice-cold water and set aside. This crisps up the spring onions and makes them curl up beautifully.

Drizzle a little olive oil over the skirt steak and season. Fry in a searingly hot pan for about 1–2 minutes on each side – a little longer if the steak is thick (though it should be quite thin). Set aside to rest.

Make the dressing. Using a pestle and mortar, pound the garlic, chilli and sugar until you have a smooth paste. Add the lime juice, fish sauce and 1 tablespoon water, mix together and set aside.

Finely grate the papaya and mango. I find the grating attachment on a mandolin the best way to do this, but if the fruit is a little soft, it is best to finely slice the fruit and julienne it by hand.

When ready to serve, toss the papaya, mango, spring onions and herbs with the dressing. Slice the beef against the grain as thinly as possible and serve alongside, garnished with the sesame seeds, crispy fried shallots, peanuts and chilli.

Tips: Skirt steak is best served rare, hence the very short cooking time. If you prefer your meat more well done, opt for a cut such as fillet.

If you would prefer to eat this without beef, it will be 221 calories per portion.

romanesco, apple and freekeh with blackened cauliflower, horseradish and dill

Cauliflower stalks are as edible and delicious as the rest of this fantastic vegetable, yet so often they end up being discarded. Here, the stalk is used to create the base of a wonderful dressing. This salad is beautifully simple and delicate.

Serves 4

Carbs 25g   Sugar 8g   Protein 9g   Fibre 6g   Fat 7.5g   Sat Fat 1g   Salt trace

100g freekeh
1 romanesco cauliflower
    (approx. 500g)
1 tablespoon olive oil
1 pink lady apple
squeeze of lemon juice
25g dill, to garnish
salt and freshly ground black
    pepper

For the dressing
100g cauliflower stalk (see
    method)
2 tablespoons yogurt
1½ tablespoons cider vinegar
1 tablespoon olive oil
5g dill
3 teaspoons grated horseradish
    (fresh or from a jar)
juice of ½ lemon

Preheat the oven to 200°C/gas mark 6.

Cover the freekeh with water, bring to the boil and simmer for about 20–25 minutes until tender. Drain, rinse under cold water and set aside.

Slice the cauliflower in half and remove and reserve the inner stalk. Break up the two halves into little florets and place on a baking tray, drizzle with the olive oil and season generously with salt and pepper. Roast for 10–15 minutes, checking a couple of times to ensure they do not burn.

To make the dressing, place a griddle pan over a high heat and grill the cauliflower stalk until blackened all over. Don't worry if it looks burned – this is part of what gives the dressing its flavour.

Transfer to a blender with all the other dressing ingredients and 2 tablespoons of water and blitz until completely smooth. You want the consistency of pouring cream so add a little more water if it is too thick. Season.

Cut the apple into quarters and remove the core then finely slice and dress with a squeeze of lemon juice. When the cauliflower is roasted, allow it to cool a little (or totally if you prefer it cold). Place in a bowl with the apple and freekeh and toss with the dressing. Serve garnished with dill.

summer berry sorbet salad

This recipe has a bit of fun with a berry fruit salad, piling it on top of blackberry sorbet in an ice-cream cone. The sorbet is nothing more than blitzed frozen berries and maple syrup. Genuine guilt-free indulgence!

Serves 4 calories 247 (VE and DF if using VE cones)

Carbs 40g   Sugar 28g   Protein 4.5g   Fibre 8g   Fat 6g   Sat Fat 0.5g   Salt 0.1g

300g frozen blackberries
1½ tablespoons maple syrup
½ tablespoon vanilla bean paste
50g Toasted Hazelnuts in Agave
   nectar (see page 148) plus
   1½ tablespoons to serve
100g raspberries
300g strawberries, quartered
100g blueberries
1 tablespoon icing sugar
10 mint leaves, finely chopped
juice of ½ lemon
4 waffle ice-cream cones
   (52 calories per cone)

Allow the frozen berries to defrost at room temperature for about 5 minutes, and then place them in a food-processor with the maple syrup and vanilla bean paste. Pulse until silky smooth and transfer to a Tupperware box. Dot the toasted hazelnuts over the surface and press them into the sorbet. Freeze for 6–7 hours or overnight if possible.

When ready to serve, put the fresh berries into a bowl, sprinkle over the icing sugar, toss to coat and leave for at least 10 minutes.

Take the sorbet from the freezer and allow to soften a little. Just before assembling the cones, add the mint and lemon juice to the fruit salad.

Pile some fruit salad into an ice-cream cone, top with a couple of scoops of sorbet and finish with another spoonful of berries and their juices. Decorate with extra toasted hazelnuts.

Tip: you need a very wide ice-cream cone to fit everything in; try buying from an ice cream shop if you have difficulty finding them.

roasted plum and popped quinoa breakfast salad with yogurt

As summer sunsets fade into the horizon for the last time and my appetite begins to crave more warming autumnal dishes, this breakfast could not be more perfect.

Serves 4 calories 253 V

Carbs 39g   Sugar 30g   Protein 6.5g   Fibre 5.5g   Fat 7g   Sat Fat 1g   Salt 0.1g

6 medium ripe plums (about 700g), mixed varieties if you can find them
1 vanilla pod
1 cinnamon stick
1 star anise
¼ teaspoon freshly grated nutmeg
1 teaspoon soft brown sugar
1 tablespoon agave nectar

To serve
130g Popped Quinoa and Sour Cherry Granola (see page 134)
4 tablespoons natural yogurt

Preheat the oven to 190°C/gas mark 5.

Halve each plum and remove the stone. Slice bigger plums into six and smaller ones into four. Pack into a roasting dish just big enough to fit the wedges in a single layer.

Slice the vanilla pod in half, remove the seeds and add these to the dish – don't worry if they are in clumps, they will disperse later on. Add the pod, cinnamon stick, star anise, nutmeg, sugar, agave nectar and 100ml of water. Toss to combine and roast for 20 minutes (if your plums are not very ripe, they may need a little longer).

Serve sprinkled with the popped quinoa and sour cherry granola, a generous spoonful of natural yogurt and the juices from the roasting tin.

popped quinoa and sour cherry granola

Egg whites are used here in place of oil to act as a binding agent, making this granola much lighter and more delicate than most. This recipe makes a decent amount so keep it in an airtight container.

Makes about 600g
(124 calories per 30g portion)

 calories 124 DF V

Carbs 15g   Sugar 7.5g   Protein 3.5g   Fibre 1.5g   Fat 5g   Sat Fat 0.5g   Salt trace

80g puffed quinoa
30g spelt puffs
120g jumbo oats
½ teaspoon ground cinnamon
I quantity Toasted Hazelnuts in Agave Nectar (see page 148)
2 medium free-range egg whites
I teaspoon vanilla bean paste
60g sour cherries
60g pumpkin seeds

Preheat the oven to 130°C/gas mark I. Put the puffed quinoa, spelt puffs, jumbo oats and cinnamon into a large bowl and toss to combine. Strain the nectar from the hazelnuts and add the nuts to the bowl.

In a separate bowl, whisk together the agave hazelnut nectar, egg whites and vanilla bean paste. Add to the grains and mix gently with your hands until everything is thoroughly coated.

Divide the mixture between two baking trays, flatten into a thin layer and bake for 30 minutes, or until golden brown all over. Check a few times to ensure it is not burning or cooking unevenly. Remove from the oven and allow to cool completely. Scrape the granola off the baking trays and mix with the sour cherries and pumpkin seeds. Store in an airtight container.

chicory, blood orange and pecorino with hazelnut and agave dressing

The bitterness of a chicory leaf can be a little overwhelming, but with a bit of thoughtful balancing, this leaf comes right into its own. Here it is teamed with sweet blood orange, nutty hazelnut agave nectar and creamy pecorino. Winner winner, chicory dinner!

Serves 4

Carbs 13.5g   Sugar 11.5g   Protein 6g   Fibre 3g   Fat 13.5g   Sat Fat 2.5g   Salt 0.4g

1 head of green chicory

1 head of red chicory

10g flat-leaf parsley, finely chopped

5g chives, finely chopped

2 blood oranges

30g pecorino, shaved

50g Toasted Hazelnuts in Agave Nectar (see page 148) plus 3 teaspoons of the nectar

For the dressing

2 tablespoons blood orange juice

1 tablespoon olive oil

1 teaspoon nectar from Toasted Hazelnuts in Agave Nectar (see page 148)

1 teaspoon white wine vinegar

pinch of salt

Finely shred the chicory leaves and place in a large bowl with the parsley and chives.

Peel the blood oranges and, using a sharp knife, cut out each segment. Add to the chicory and herbs.

Mix all the dressing ingredients together and pour over the salad. Toss to ensure everything is evenly coated.

Serve topped with the shaved pecorino, agave hazelnuts and a drizzle of agave nectar.

crispy duck and pomelo

This recipe is inspired by one of the best salads I have ever had – at Hakkasan in London. The combination of zingy citrus fruits and fatty duck is sublime. This is a generous salad for indulgent appetites.

Serves 4

Carbs 10g   Sugar 11g   Protein 10g   Fibre 2.5g   Fat 8g   Sat Fat 1.5g   Salt 2.1g

1 tablespoon olive oil
1 teaspoon flour
¾ teaspoon five-spice powder
15g pine nuts
150g mixed baby leaves
1 large pink grapefruit, segmented
½ pomelo (or use 1 white grapefruit), segmented
50g radish sprouts
1 punnet of cress, trimmed
sea salt and freshly ground black pepper

For the duck
3 each star anise, cloves, bay leaves and dried red chillies
1 cinnamon stick
10 black peppercorns
1 teaspoon five-spice powder
2 duck legs, weighing about 500g

For the dressing
½ ripe plum, de-stoned and roughly chopped
3 tablespoons hoi sin sauce
1½ tablespoons soy sauce
juice of ½ lime
1 teaspoon honey

Place all the ingredients for the duck in a medium saucepan with 1 teaspoon salt and cover with water. Bring to the boil, reduce to a simmer and cook for 1 hour. Leave to cool in the water. It is a good idea, if you are organised enough, to do this step a day in advance.

To make the dressing, blitz all the ingredients together until smooth. Season to taste with salt and pepper.

When you are ready to eat, remove the skin from the duck and pull all the meat from the bone. Heat the oil in a frying pan over a high heat. Dust the duck with the flour, five-spice powder and a generous pinch of salt and pepper. When the pan is smoking hot, fry the duck until browned and crispy, about 5–7 minutes. Drain on kitchen paper. Toast the pine nuts in the same frying pan until golden.

Put the mixed leaves, grapefruit, pomelo, radish sprouts and cress in a large bowl and toss with three-quarters of the dressing. Serve topped with the duck and pine nuts, and finish with the remaining dressing. Serve immediately.

lapsang souchong salt-baked beetroot, physalis, goat's cheese and dill

Physalis is a small fruit encased in a papery lantern-like husk and is deliciously sweet and sour with a nice crunch to it. Lots of supermarkets sell it, so keep an eye out. Salt-baked beetroot is a heavenly treat and so worth the effort it takes to cook it — and you could do this a day ahead if you wish. Salads don't come more luscious than this!

Serves 4   calories 192   GF   V

Carbs 12g   Sugar 11g   Protein 10g   Fibre 3g   Fat 11g   Sat Fat 5g   Salt 3g

500g baby beetroot, use mixed varieties and colours if you can find them

500g coarse sea salt

30g lapsang souchong loose tea leaves

5 thyme sprigs, leaves picked

1 rosemary sprig, leaves picked

3 medium free-range egg whites

100g physalis, papery husk removed, halved

100g soft goat's cheese or curd

5g dill, fronds finely chopped

1½ tablespoons light, fruity extra virgin olive oil

squeeze of lemon juice

salt and freshly ground black pepper

Preheat the oven to 180°C/gas mark 4. Line a baking tray with parchment paper and place the beetroot on top.

Put the salt, tea leaves, thyme and rosemary into a food-processor and pulse until the salt is nice and fine. Add the egg whites and pulse again until you have a paste.

Gather the beetroot close together on the baking tray and completely cover with the salt mixture — there should be no gaps or holes and no beetroot visible through the layer of paste. Bake for 1 hour.

Remove from the oven and leave to cool.

When ready to use, crack open the crust with a knife and remove the beetroot. Use kitchen paper to rub away the skins and any residual salt. Quarter each beetroot.

To serve, arrange the beetroot and physalis on a large plate. Dot little spoonfuls of the soft goat's cheese all over, garnish with dill and drizzle with olive oil. Finish with a squeeze of lemon juice and a pinch of salt and pepper, and then go and show it off!

dressings, condiments and pickles

A dressing can make the difference between a mediocre and a magnificent salad, and so it makes sense to be armed with a few recipes that will lead you down the path to success. These are not your typical dressings. Much more than traditional (calorie laden) oil and vinegar, they are jam-packed with flavour, each created to transform the salad it adorns. Oil is not always the main component. Instead you will find dressings such as the creamy Blue Cheese Dressing, with a yogurt base, or the Roasted Red Pepper, Basil and Chilli Dressing, which gives you a hit of nutrition as well as flavour. Herbs play a starring role in the Salsa Verde Dressing and this, like the roasted red pepper one, the Chermoula and the Pomegranate, Mint and Coriander Dressing, is suitable for freezing: simply pop tablespoon measures into ice-cube trays for a ready-made dressing whenever you need it.

These recipes take everyday salad ingredients such as cucumbers, tomatoes, onions and peppers and give them a makeover. The difference between a raw and pickled onion is insurmountable; onions, when pickled, become an integral part of a salad rather than overpowering it. Ricotta is unbelievably easy to make and adds a touch of indulgence to salads. The flavoured cider vinegar is a great all-rounder to have on hand, and while the recipe in this chapter calls for tarragon, thyme and lemon, you could get creative here and try out your own flavours.

There are lots of ways to sterilise jars, but the quickest and easiest is to simply wash them in soapy water then rinse thoroughly with boiling water from the kettle. Don't forget to do the lids too, and be careful to not burn your hands.

lemon and lime vinaigrette

This is a wonderfully light, zesty and refreshing dressing. A great all-rounder and it's worth making a batch of to keep handy in your fridge.

Makes 125ml, 44 calories per tablespoon

Carbs 1.5g Sugar 1.5g Protein 0g Fibre 0g Fat 4g Sat Fat 0.6g Salt 0.01g

1 lemon
1 lime
3 tablespoons extra virgin olive oil
2 teaspoons agave nectar
1 teaspoon Dijon mustard
salt and freshly ground black pepper

Use a potato peeler to peel three strips of zest from both the lemon and lime, avoiding the white pith. Slice lengthways as thinly as possible and then finely chop.

Squeeze the juice from the fruit into a small bowl or jar and add the olive oil, agave nectar, Dijon mustard and a small pinch of salt and pepper. Whisk together until you have a light emulsion.

Refrigerate until needed. It will keep in your fridge for up to 2 weeks, and the flavour will intensify over time as the rind infuses the dressing.

salsa verde dressing

Salsa verde would normally be seen accompanying simply cooked fresh fish. However, with a flavour so powerful and special, its uses are endless and have included it here as an amazing salad dressing. It is a great way to use up herbs in your fridge, too – experiment with different kinds, but always use a sufficient quantity of parsley to give it a good base flavour.

Makes 325g, 33 calories per tablespoon

Carbs 0g   Sugar 0g   Protein 0.5g   Fibre 0g   Fat 3.5g   Sat Fat 0.5g   Salt 0.2g

1 garlic clove
4 cornichons
2 tablespoons capers
5 anchovies
40g flat-leaf parsley
20g mint
10g dill
10g tarragon
zest and juice of 1 lemon
6 tablespoons olive oil
3 tablespoons red wine vinegar
1½ tablespoons Dijon mustard
salt and freshly ground black pepper

Finely grate or chop the garlic and place in a mini food-processor. Add the cornichons, capers and anchovies and pulse until roughly chopped. Add the remaining ingredients, along with 2 tablespoons of water, and pulse a few more times to roughly chop the herbs. Season to taste and refrigerate until needed.

Stored in the fridge, it will keep for up to 1 week.

chermoula dressing

The intense flavour of this adds a real depth to any salad, and can be a real 'Jack-of-all-trades' kind of condiment: use it to marinate meat, chicken or fish; as a sauce for pasta; or spread it on crusty bread to make the base of a cracking sandwich.

Makes 200ml, 18 calories per tablespoon

Carbs 0.6g   Sugar 0.6g   Protein 0.2g   Fibre 0.3g   Fat 1.5g   Sat Fat 0.2g   Salt 0.2g

I teaspoon cumin
I garlic clove, roughly chopped
1½ teaspoons paprika
½ teaspoon chilli flakes
I pickled roasted red pepper (see page 154)
   or use shop bought, finely chopped
30g coriander, finely chopped
15g flat-leaf parsley, finely chopped
I tablespoon olive oil
juice of ½ lemon
juice of ½ lime
salt and freshly ground black pepper

Toast the cumin in a dry frying pan for a couple of minutes until aromatic but not colouring. Pound using a pestle and mortar until roughly ground.

Add the garlic, paprika, chilli flakes and a generous pinch of salt and pepper and grind until you have quite a dry paste. Add the remaining ingredients and pound just long enough to give you a chunky, textured dressing. Taste for seasoning, and let out with a little water if it is too thick.

pomegranate, mint and coriander dressing

So gorgeous that it transforms a humble bowl of leaves into something special.

Makes 150ml, 34 calories per tablespoon   (VE if using agave nectar)

Carbs 2.5g   Sugar 2.3g   Protein 0.3g   Fibre 0.3g   Fat 2.5g   Sat Fat 0.3g   Salt 0.1g

I teaspoon cumin seeds
2 tablespoons olive oil
1½ tablespoons pomegranate molasses
I tablespoon Dijon mustard
½ teaspoon agave nectar or honey
juice of I lime and zest of ½
50g pomegranate seeds
5g each mint and coriander, finely
   chopped
salt and freshly ground black pepper

Toast the cumin seeds in a dry frying pan for a couple of minutes. Pound using a pestle and mortar and grind to a rough powder.

Transfer to a bowl, add the remaining ingredients and whisk together. Season to taste. Refrigerate until needed. It will keep for up to I week.

roasted red pepper, basil and chilli dressing

You won't believe this has only 8 calories per tablespoon. Low calorie does not equal bland or boring; this little gem is anything but.

Makes about 220g, 8 calories per tablespoon

Carbs 1g   Sugar 1g   Protein 0.3g   Fibre 0.6g   Fat 0g   Sat Fat 0g   Salt 0.01g

2 red peppers (or use Pickled Roasted Red
    Peppers, see page 154)
1 red chilli
20g basil
1½ tablespoons sherry vinegar
salt and freshly ground black pepper

Preheat the oven to 240°C/gas mark 9.

Place the peppers on a baking tray
and roast for about 35 minutes, until
blackened. Ten minutes before they are
ready, add the chilli to the tray.

Transfer to a bowl, cover with clingfilm
and leave until cool enough to handle.

Tear each pepper in half, reserving as
much of their natural oil as possible, and
remove the seeds. Place into the bowl of a
food-processor along with the chilli, basil,
sherry vinegar and any oil from the roasted
peppers. Blitz until smooth and season with
salt and pepper.

The dressing will keep in the fridge for up
to 1 week and is suitable for freezing.

Tip: If using pickled peppers, omit the first
three steps and the sherry vinegar.

sumac, chilli and lemon yogurt dressing

Not only is yogurt a great vehicle for flavour, used in a dressing it makes any salad feel more substantial.

Makes 80ml / Serves 4, 26 calories per serving

Carbs 1.5g   Sugar 1.5g   Protein 1g   Fibre 0g   Fat 2g   Sat Fat 0.5g   Salt 0.1g

60ml natural yogurt
½ tablespoon olive oil
zest and juice of ½ lemon
1½ teaspoons sumac
½ teaspoon mild chilli powder
salt and freshly ground black pepper

Mix all the ingredients together and season
to taste.

Tip: The 'use by' date on the yogurt you
use will indicate how long the dressing will
keep in the fridge.

toasted hazelnuts in agave nectar

A recipe doesn't come simpler than this, and once you have made it, I guarantee you'll want a supply of these in your cupboard forever. The intense flavour of the agave works brilliantly in dressings. Feel free to experiment with different nuts, too.

Makes a 250ml jar, 27 calories per kernel
24 calories per teaspoon of nectar

| Carbs 0.2g | Sugar 0.2g | Protein 0.7g | Fibre 0.3g | Fat 2.5g | Sat Fat 0.2g | Salt 0g |

Equipment
250ml sterilised Kilner or preserving jar

100g blanched hazelnuts
150ml agave nectar

Toast the hazelnuts in a dry frying pan until golden all over.

Immediately transfer to a 250ml sterilised jar and pour over the agave nectar to cover. Seal and allow the flavours to infuse for 2–3 days before using.

The nuts will keep, sealed in an airtight jar, almost indefinitely.

blue cheese dressing

There is no reason why indulgent ingredients such as creamy blue cheese shouldn't find their way into a book of low-calorie recipes. This dressing is proof that you can have your cake — or, in this case, cheese — and eat it too!

Serves 4, 52 calories per portion

| Carbs 1g | Sugar 1g | Protein 2g | Fibre 0g | Fat 4.5g | Sat Fat 3g | Salt 0.4g |

35g strong soft blue cheese, e.g. Roquefort
2 tablespoons soured cream
2 tablespoons buttermilk
1½ tablespoons lemon juice
½ teaspoon Worcestershire sauce
1 tablespoon chopped chives
salt and freshly ground black pepper

In a bowl, mash the cheese a little so that it is nice and smooth. Add the remaining ingredients and mix well. Season to taste.

This dressing will keep in the fridge for 4–5 days, and freezes well. To make this vegetarian, use Dolcelatte cheese and omit the Worcestershire sauce.

sweet pickled red onions

These are an amazing store-cupboard standby and enhance almost any salad to which they are added.

Makes a 500ml jar, 45 calories per ¼ jar

. . . .

Carbs 9.5g   Sugar 8g   Protein 0.8g   Fibre 1.5g   Fat 0g   Sat Fat 0g   Salt 0.7g

. . . .

Equipment
500ml sterilised Kilner or preserving jar

2 red onions
230ml cider vinegar
50g sugar
¾ tablespoon black peppercorns
1½ teaspoons salt
3 dried chillies
4 thyme sprigs

Peel, halve and slice the red onions as thinly as possible (use the slicer attachment of a food-processor or mandolin if you have one) and place in a sterilised jar.

Heat the remaining ingredients in a small saucepan until almost boiling. Stir gently to dissolve the sugar, then remove from the heat and allow to cool completely.

Pour over the onions and leave for 2 or 3 days before using. Refrigerate once opened. They will keep for up to 4 weeks once opened(?).

homemade ricotta

Ricotta adds the most delicate touch of indulgence to a salad, is unashamedly decadent and couldn't be easier to make: it is as simple as boiling milk and straining it. If you are feeling creative, play around with the flavours you use to infuse the milk.

Makes 325g, 73 calories per 25g (see tip)

Carbs 5g Sugar 5g Protein 0.7g Fibre 0g Fat 4g Sat Fat 2.5g Salt 1.9g

Equipment
muslin cloth
500ml sterilised Kilner or
    preserving jar

1.5 litres whole milk
4 tablespoons lemon juice
1½ tablespoons Maldon sea salt
1 thyme sprig
a few peppercorns
olive oil

For the bouquet garni
10 thyme sprigs
1 tablespoon black peppercorns
1½ teaspoons coriander seeds
¼ celery stick, roughly chopped

Securely tie up all the ingredients for the bouquet garni in a small square of muslin.

Pour the milk into a large pan, add the bouquet garni and very gently heat until steaming and almost boiling (about 20–30 minutes), then remove from the heat.

Remove the bouquet garni, add the lemon juice and stir very gently. The milk will separate and curdle immediately. Add the salt and gently stir one more time. Allow to settle for a few minutes.

Place a sieve lined with two large squares of muslin over a large bowl. Pour in the curdled milk and leave to strain for about 30 minutes.

Scoop the muslin cloth up and tie with a long piece of string. Suspend it over a bowl, tying it to a handle on your kitchen cupboard or the tap in your sink, and leave to strain for 2–3 hours. Leave it overnight (in the fridge) if you prefer it firmer (see tip).

Remove the ricotta from the muslin, cut into cubes and place in the preserving jar with the thyme and peppercorns. Pour in enough oil to totally cover. It will keep for up to 2 weeks in the fridge.

Tip: Create different textures of ricotta by varying the length of time and how you let it strain. For a softer ricotta, leave to strain in the sieve for about an hour. Use this ricotta as a dip that's delicious with crudités, for example. Leaving it a little longer will give you a slightly firmer texture, spreadable like cream cheese. Play around with it and have some fun!

pickled chargrilled cucumber

Chargrilling these cucumbers before pickling creates the most amazing flavour. They are a favourite in my house, and a great addition to the table as a garnish at almost every meal.

Makes a 1-litre jar, 29 calories per 100g

Carbs 5g   Sugar 5g   Protein 0.7g   Fibre 0g   Fat 4g   Sat Fat 2.5g   Salt 1.9g

Equipment

1-litre sterilised Kilner or
    preserving jar

500ml cider vinegar
1½ tablespoons salt
60g caster sugar
9 Lebanese cucumbers or 2
    normal cucumbers, halved
1 tablespoon pink peppercorns
    (or use black peppercorns)
3 dill sprigs

Put the vinegar, salt and sugar in a pan and bring to the boil. Stir to ensure the sugar is dissolved then remove from the heat and allow to cool completely.

Place a griddle pan over a high heat and, when smoking hot, add the cucumbers. Chargrill the cucumbers until lightly blackened on all sides, about 20 minutes. Keep an eye on them and turn as they cook. Allow to cool, then slice thinly (no thicker than 4mm) on the diagonal.

Put the cucumber slices in a sterilised jar, layering them with the peppercorns and dill. Pour the cooled pickling liquor over the cucumbers, seal the jar and leave for a couple of days.

Once opened, store in the fridge. They will keep for up to 2 months.

Tip: In summer, chargrill the cucumbers on the barbecue before pickling for an even more intense flavour.

pickled roasted red peppers

These are a genuine treat preserved in a jar!

Makes a 750ml jar, 63 calories per ½ pepper

Carbs 4g   Sugar 3.5g   Protein 0.6g   Fibre 1.5g   Fat 5g   Sat Fat 0.7g   Salt 0.9g

8 large red peppers (or a mix of colours)
1 tablespoon Maldon sea salt
¾ tablespoon caster sugar
5–6 leafy thyme sprigs, leaves picked
60ml sherry vinegar
3 bay leaves
2 teaspoons black peppercorns

Preheat the oven to 240°C/gas mark 9. Place the peppers on a baking tray and roast for 30–35 minutes, until nicely charred but still holding their shape. Remove, transfer to a bowl, cover with clingfilm and allow to cool.

Above a sieve placed over a medium bowl, gently peel the papery skin from the peppers, tear each in half and remove and discard the stalk and seeds. Allow the natural oil from the peppers to gather in the bowl and measure out 100ml.

Sprinkle the salt, sugar and thyme over the peppers and mix to thoroughly coat them. Pour the vinegar into a 750ml sterilised jar, then add the peppers, layering with the bay leaves and peppercorns and gently pressing down to ensure there are no air bubbles. There should be a little space at the top of the jar. Press the peppers down once more and fill the jar with the 100ml of oil from the peppers. Seal and leave for a few days before using. The peppers will keep for up to 1 month in the fridge.

tarragon, thyme and lemon vinegar

This flavoured vinegar is wonderfully aromatic and used in place of other vinegars, such as cider or white wine. It is a great way to add another layer of flavour to a dressing.

Makes a 250ml bottle, 1 calorie per 100ml

Carbs 0g   Sugar 0g   Protein 0g   Fibre 0g   Fat 0g   Sat Fat 0g   Salt 0g

250ml cider vinegar
3 thyme sprigs
3 tarragon sprigs
pared zest of ¼ lemon, finely sliced
1 teaspoon pink peppercorns

Bring the cider vinegar to the boil and pour over the herbs, lemon and peppercorns in a 250ml sterilised bottle. Seal and allow the flavours to infuse for 2 weeks before using.

pickled smoked cherry tomatoes

Home smoking genuinely is one of the easiest things to do; you probably already have all the equipment you need. You can get creative by using different types of tea for flavour, adding dry spices for aroma, and by smoking whatever takes your fancy — cheese, vegetables, fish, poultry, meat, or, in this case, tomatoes. When they are pickled they harden slightly, taking on the most beautiful texture: tomatoes don't get more special than this.

Makes a 1-litre jar, 21 calories per 100g

Carbs 4g   Sugar 4g   Protein 0.5g   Fibre 1g   Fat 0g   Sat Fat 0g   Salt 0.7g

Equipment
1-litre sterilised Kilner or
   preserving jar

For smoking
a large handful of dry rice
3 tablespoons loose lapsang
   souchong tea leaves

700g cherry tomatoes, use
   mixed colours if you can find
   them
3 or 4 thyme sprigs
1 oregano sprig
1 tablespoon peppercorns
1 teaspoon lapsang souchong
   loose tea leaves

For the pickling liquid
450ml cider vinegar
4 tablespoons sugar
1½ tablespoons salt

First prepare your 'smoker'. Line a frying pan or wok with three layers of foil and scatter the rice and tea leaves on top. Place over a high heat. Don't worry if the rice pops and blackens a little — this is totally normal.

Put the tomatoes on a wire rack big enough to rest on top of the wok or frying pan. When the smoke begins to billow from the pan, place the rack on top and cover this with another two layers of foil, making sure the foil traps in all the smoke. Be careful not to burn yourself when doing this. Smoke for 10 minutes, then remove from the heat and set aside until the tomatoes are completely cool. It is a good idea to put the pan outside while it is still smoking.

Meanwhile, make the pickling liquid. Bring the cider vinegar, sugar and salt to the boil, stir to dissolve the sugar, then remove from the heat and leave to cool completely.

When the tomatoes are cool, transfer to a sterilised jar, along with the thyme, oregano, peppercorns, tea leaves and pickling liquor. Seal and leave for a few days before using.

This pickle will keep unopened for 6 months.
Once opened, refrigerate and use within 2 weeks.

index

acknowledgements

It was such a privilege to be given the opportunity to write one book, but to be trusted with another means so much to me. I am very grateful to Kyle Cathie for believing in me, and for giving me such an amazing platform from which I can continue following one of my biggest dreams.

Claire, my editor, you have patience and advice in abundance, and are always so helpful and reassuring. It has been a joy doing another book together, and I can't thank you enough for being so open to my ideas and visions.

Laura Edwards and Tabitha Hawkins, our days of shooting were a masterclass in how fun a day's work should be. Laura, your natural and very unique touch graces every photograph in this book, and Tabs, I can't thank you enough for going over and above with every round of props you brought to the studio. Louise Leffler, once again thank you for designing such a beautiful book. Together, you have all brought my ideas to life in a way I couldn't even have imagined. I can't tell you how grateful I am for that!

I was blessed with fantastic assistants – Becks, Laura and Sophie; thank you for keeping my head above water every day we worked together. Sorry for being so utterly messy and chaotic!

To my chief team of tasters – Rich, Mikey and Sammy; yet again you have all contributed massively to the success of these recipes, although I know Mikey would add more salt and chilli to them all if he had his way! All of my family, in Ireland and in Lichfield, were involved from start to finish, as they are in everything I do. Kate and Freda, I know I can always turn to you guys for advice and input, as well as being a helping hand to clear the fridge – we have had many a feast! To Polly, GT, Tone and Meels; you were fantastic guinea pigs when I needed you and I hope the flavour of a pickled smoked tomato will always be a fond memory!

All four of my brothers and sisters are among my closest and most cherished friends. Everything I do, I do with you all, and there are simply not enough words to articulate how lucky I feel to have you. Mam, you are, without a doubt, my biggest inspiration; thank you for never tiring of my continual requests for help and advice. You have been so instrumental in helping me build this book, always encouraging me when I felt like I was failing and showing me how to see the positive in everything. To You, Gary, Mark, Liz, Grace, John, Barry, Johnny and Beth; thank you for always being by my side, even though there is a great big sea between us.

Dad, even though you are no longer with us, I know you are perched on my shoulder, silently guiding me through this life that you were tragically and prematurely taken from. Everything I do, I do with you in my heart and in my mind and I miss you everyday.

To my gorgeous daughter Elsie, when you are old enough to read this, you will be able to tell me that, 'No Mum, I would much prefer you to play with me rather than test recipes'. But, for now, thank you Little Girl for being the angel you are and allowing me to spend time on books when, really, you would prefer I was spending it with you!

To Rich, I think there came a point when I was making you eat salad for breakfast, lunch and dinner – there is not a single detail of this book that you haven't been involved in. It is suffice to say that I couldn't do any of this without you (even though you would argue that I could!). It is a journey, writing a book, and I am not sure I could sail that journey quite so successfully if it wasn't for you being by my side. Thank you for dreaming my dreams, and for keeping me going. Fancy a Niçoise for dinner?!